FINER GROUNDS

Pursued:

God's Plan for Intimacy in Marriage

A Study of the Song of Solomon

Lacy Crowell

Dedication

To Jonathan: my best friend, my love, my
partner in all things. Thank you
for pursuing me with the love of Christ. It
is my great joy to be yours.
"I have found him whom my soul loves."
Song of Solomon 3:4

To my darling kiddos: Know that I pray
for you and your future spouses daily. May
your future marriages grow and thrive as
you pursue your Savior first and foremost.
Choose each other, and love and laugh,
every day. I love you!

Finer Grounds | Pursued: God's Plan for Intimacy in Marriage

Copyright © 2021 by Kaio Publications, Inc. All Rights Reserved.

All rights reserved. No portion of this book may be reproduced in any form for commercial purposes without the written permission of the Publisher.

Published by Kaio Publications, Inc.
PO Box 118
Spring Hill, TN 37174
www.kaiopublications.org

ISBN: 978-1-952955-02-0

Unless noted otherwise Scripture is taken from NASB is taken from the New American Standard Bible, copyright © 1960, 1962, 1963, 1968, 1971, 1972, 1973, 1975, 1977, 1995 by The Lockman Foundation. Used by permission.

Book edited by Tonja McRady

Design and layout: D.J. Smith, Nashville, TN & Ben Giselbach, Cleveland, TN

Printed in the United States of America.

Contents

	About Lacy	6
	What Is Finer Grounds?	7
Chapter 1	Introduction to Song of Solomon	9
Chapter 2	The Courtship	17
Chapter 3	Love's Consummation	27
Chapter 4	The Getaway	35
Chapter 5	The Dream	43
Chapter 6	Remembering the Wedding Night	49
Chapter 7	The Honeymoon Is Over	57
Chapter 8	A Different Perspective	67
Chapter 9	Together Again	75
Chapter 10	Solomon Delights in His Wife	81
Chapter 11	The Romantic Rendezvous	89
Chapter 12	Happily Ever After	99
Chapter 13	After "I Do:" Barriers to Intimacy	107
	Recommended Reading	127
	Works Cited	131

About Lacy

Lacy Crowell is a Licensed Marriage and Family Therapist with Focus Mental Health Services. She and her husband, Jonathan, have been married for 20 years and have four precious children: Re'Elle, Ariana, Mya, and Jathan, whom Lacy has been blessed to homeschool. She has a passion for helping her brethren understand God's pattern for the family, and in particular helping to grow and strengthen marriages according to God's design. Lacy received an Associate of Arts in Bible from the Bear Valley Bible Institute and completed both her undergraduate and graduate studies at Amridge University. She has been privileged to speak for women and teen girls in venues both domestic and foreign and is the author of the book *Proclaimed: Jesus the Messiah*, a Study of the Gospel of Mark. She and her family worship with the Garriott Rd. church of Christ in Enid, Oklahoma where Jonathan serves as the Youth and Family Minister.

What Is Finer Grounds?

Finer Grounds is a verse by verse, chapter by chapter, book by book, meaty, deep digging study of God's Word. Enrich your personal Bible time or study with a group of ladies. Thought-provoking questions help you reach new levels of faith. Studies are thoroughly researched and passages are expertly explained. Lessons are structured in 13-week (one quarter) segments so you can easily share them with your ladies' Bible class.

Chapter 1
Introduction

At this exact moment, girls and young women all around the world are dreaming of their "Prince Charming." They are wondering what he will look like, what he will sound like, and what his name will be. They are picturing their wedding and even imagining what they will name their children. In today's culture, they may have even already created a "Wedding Dream Board" on Pinterest as they sigh over the perfect future life that they just know is waiting for them. Unfortunately, for many Christian women, this fairy tale is short-lived in real life. It doesn't take long for many women to become disillusioned with the realities of marriage. In fact, my husband and I once engaged in pre-marital counseling with a couple that almost didn't even make it to the wedding because they had their first argument and feared this meant their marriage was doomed.

After the wedding, it doesn't take long for reality to set in. This reality could be anything from infertility to a pornography addiction, or even just the task of melding two lives together. It doesn't take long to begin to wonder, "What went wrong?" Some women simply resign themselves to an "OK" marriage because they just don't know what else to do. Others begin to feel that they are somehow fundamentally flawed because they are struggling with their marriage when it seems to come so easily for everyone else. They have dreamed of this relationship for their entire lives--how can it be so hard? Unfortunately, some women even begin to question whether they married "the one" when hardship hits.

I believe that one of the primary reasons Christian women struggle so desperately with their marriages today is because we are inundated with the world's view of sex and relationships on a daily basis, even when we strive to protect our hearts and minds from ungodly influences. In our hyper-sexualized culture, the mantra "sex sells" has overtaken every aspect of media, from scantily clad women in commercials dancing around the latest vehicle model to giant billboards promoting XXX video stores as we drive down the road. This, along with instantaneous internet access on every device in our homes, has led to an epidemic of pornography use. Pornography has devastating effects on sexuality and relationships and leaves many women (even Christian women) feeling that they just cannot compete or have the beautiful sexual relationship of which they dreamed.

With the world's view of sexuality and marriage being thrown at us every time we turn on the television or walk out our front door, what are we to do? When many of us face the very real disillusionment of our marriages or even our sexual relationships with our husbands not being easy and perfect all the time, where do we turn? Fortunately, God knows us and our needs better than we ourselves do, and in His great wisdom He has provided for us. The Song of Solomon is a beautiful and at times graphically detailed picture of God's design and intent for marriage. Through an in-depth, practical study of Solomon and his marriage to the Shulamite woman, we will gain a deeper understanding of the beauty of God's design for marriage and the sexual relationship. We will learn how to be intentional with our husbands and how to embrace our God-given sexual relationship in a way that will lead to greater intimacy in every aspect of marriage. We will see that, while no person and no marriage is perfect, it is possible to achieve our fairy tale relationship by following God's design. Join us as we study *Pursued: God's Plan for Intimacy in Marriage.*

Before You Begin:
Consider your current comfort level with discussing sex and sexuality with your spouse: Is this something that you find difficult? Consider your current comfort level with discussing sex and sexuality with your sisters in Christ: Is this something that you find difficult? Consider your current beliefs regarding sex and sexuality.

Think About It:
What does it say about the importance of emotional and sexual intimacy in marriage that God has given us an entire book dedicated to it? In what ways, if any, do you feel the world has influenced your view of marriage or sexuality? Why is it important to discuss Biblical sexuality as sisters in Christ? How does Titus 2:3-5 apply?

About the Song of Solomon

Before we begin digging into the text, it's necessary to lay some groundwork concerning the Song of Solomon. We will do that by considering the authorship, title, uniqueness, and style of the text. By understanding the literary context of the book, we will gain a deeper understanding of what the Song of Songs means and God's purpose in preserving this important book for us today.

Song of Solomon: Authorship

Starting in verse 1, the text states, "The Song of Songs, which is Solomon's." This clearly identifies Solomon as the author, although there are some who will argue that the author is anonymous, and this statement simply means the book is about Solomon rather than written by him. That being said, there is tremendous internal evidence as to Solomon's authorship. First of all, Solomon is mentioned by name seven times in the book: 1:1, 1:5, 3:7, 3:9, 3:11, 8:11, 8:12. Second, the artful nature of the book itself lends to Solomon's authorship. Within the Song of Solomon there are 20 species of exotic plants named, 15 exotic animals, and many varied geographical locations mentioned (Petrillo 254). It would have taken a great deal of wealth and freedom to experience the vast amount of travel required to familiarize oneself with so many locations, plants, and animals, and Solomon's status as the richest and wisest king of all time would leave him ideally placed for such travel. Additionally, the sheer excess and luxury referenced throughout the book regarding items such as rare spices and perfumes could easily be attributed to the wealth and abundance Israel knew under Solomon's rule (Garrett 352).

Song of Solomon: Title

The title, while seeming plain and redundant, is actually quite beautiful when one understands the Hebrew language of the time. While frequently translated as "The Song of Solomon," a more accurate translation is "The Song of Songs." While in English we use suffixes such as "est" to indicate an increase of worth or importance, in ancient Hebrew they used redundancy. For instance, when the well-known phrase "vanity of vanities" is used in Ecclesiastes 1:2 and 12:8, Solomon is saying that a life not in obedience to the Almighty God is the vainest life imaginable. This means that the Song of Songs is the greatest song, the best song, the most excellent song (Garrett 348).

During his lifetime, King Solomon wrote over 3,000 proverbs and 1,000 songs, yet out of all of them he believed that the Song of Songs was the best (Petrillo 252). Out of all the guidance and insight Solomon shared throughout his lifetime, in his divinely granted wisdom he believed his greatest was this short, eight-chapter book on the beauty of marital intimacy.

Uniqueness

The Song of Songs is unique in Scripture for a variety of reasons. First of all, except for a metaphorical reference in 8:6 there is not a specific mention of God found in the entire book. Out of all Scripture, the Song of Solomon and Esther are the only two books that do not mention God. Additionally, it is one of only 10 Old Testament books (Judges, Ruth, Ezra, Esther, Ecclesiastes, Lamentations, Obadiah, Jonah and Zephaniah) not directly quoted in the New Testament (Petrillo 258).

Additionally, the Song of Solomon was part of the Megilloth, a collection of Old Testament Scriptures that were read during the Jewish feasts, along with Ruth, Lamentations, Ecclesiastes and Esther (Elwell and Beitzel 1433). Each year, the Jews would read the Song of Solomon during the Passover (Elwell and Beitzel 1433). This makes the Song of Solomon one of the most publicly taught of all the Old Testament Scriptures. Quite ironic considering that for Christians it is one of the least taught, particularly in public forums.

A final unique characteristic of this book is the word usage found within. There are 47 different Hebrew words found in the Song of Solomon which are not found anywhere else in Scripture (Petrillo 266). Additionally, there are another 96 Hebrew words that are used 10 times or less in the rest of Scripture (Petrillo 266). This makes the poetic language of the Song of Songs uniquely beautiful within God's Word.

Style and Cast of Characters

The Song of Solomon is unique in that it is written as a beautiful play, detailing Solomon's courtship, wedding, and early marriage to his Shulammite bride. As we study the text, we will gain a deeper insight into this mysterious Shulammite woman: who she was, what lifestyle she lived, and how she came to be the wife of one of the most powerful men of her time. Within the text we see various speeches made by both Solomon and his bride. Additionally, we see refrains simply labeled as "chorus." Many believe that the chorus is comprised of the bride's friends, perhaps even the daughters of Jerusalem that we see mentioned in the text (Petrillo 271). Each speech is labeled according to the speaker, which helps the reader understand the context of what is being said.

As we begin our study of the Song of Solomon, keep in mind its unique format and purpose. In the entirety of Scripture, it is the only book that gives us a detailed, intimate look at God's design for intimacy in marriage. In both 2:16 and 6:3 a powerful phrase is found, "My beloved is mine, and I am his." We will see Solomon and the Shulammite glory in each other, we will see them make mistakes that push each other away, and then we will see the beauty of their reconciliation. Yet through it all, she is her beloved's, and he is hers. Sisters, if you are married, you are your beloved's and he is yours. Matthew 19:6 states, "What therefore God has joined together, let not man separate." Let us learn together how to glory in our husbands. Let us learn how to rectify and move beyond hurts and celebrate together the beautiful intimacy that God has designed specifically for marriage.

Chapter 2
The Courtship

As we begin our look at the text, the Song of Songs opens by describing the foundation of the relationship between Solomon and his Shulammite bride. We are given a behind-the-scenes peek into how they met, what her life was like before her Prince Charming swooped in and carried her off to his palace, as well as how Solomon and the Shulammite each prepare for their wedding emotionally and physically. We also see Solomon comforting his bride-to-be regarding her personal insecurities, as well as calming her fears regarding what it will be like to be married to him.

Before You Begin:
Think back to your own wedding day. Write down what you remember about how you felt and what you were thinking. How did you prepare physically and emotionally for your wedding? How did you prepare for your wedding night? What do you wish you had known then that you know now?

Read Chapter 1:1-8

For many, the beginning of the Song of Songs is shocking, as it is a clear and passionate statement of physical desire not by the man, but by the Shulammite woman. She begins the dialogue by stating that she desires the kisses of her beloved. She then goes on to describe a depth to her feelings which exceeds pure physical passion. She states that his love is better than wine, his oils are fragrant, and the virgins love him. She is shouting her triumph to the world, that she has found a man who is to be desired above all, one who makes all the other maidens look at her with jealousy.

In the Hebrew culture of the time, "wine" was a phrase used in reference to any major celebration (Dillow 13). In this context, the Shulammite is saying that her beloved brings her more joy and excitement than any party or celebration ever could. Along these lines, oils and fragrances will be a common theme throughout the Song. These were a sign of wealth and prosperity, and within an intimate relationship a sign of effort to be appealing to one's lover. This would be the same as a man wearing cologne today––he has put forth the effort to smell nice for her, with the result that she's becoming intoxicated with the thought of him.

She concludes this speech with relaying that she has run away with the king, that he has brought her into his chambers. As we will see later, this is in reference to Solomon plucking her from her menial, labor-intensive life in the country and whisking her away to a palatial life as his bride. When it speaks of his chambers it seems there is a two-fold meaning as the Hebrew word for "brought" here can also mean "to come," meaning future tense (Strong #H935). She has been whisked away from her country life of menial labor and brought to his palace home, but it also seems to be portraying her

Chapter 2 The Courtship 19

anticipation of her wedding night, coming into Solomon's bed as his wife.

Sadly, it has been my experience that what was breath-taking, exciting, consuming before marriage becomes rote, boring, routine, and an obligation after marriage for many women. The sexual desire of our betrotheds, when he would hold our hands, place his arms possessively around us, or even gaze into our eyes would speed up our pulse and send our hearts racing and our knees to quaking before marriage. Yet after marriage oftentimes their touch, their caress, their kiss is seen as an inconvenience to our day, or even worse as evidence that they are selfish and sex crazed.

Sisters, this mentality is death to our marriages. If you haven't done so before, take the time to really sit down and visit with your husband about what sex means to him. Do so with an open mind, and really listen to what he has to say. You may be shocked to learn how intertwined his sexual desire and emotional need for you are. To him, they are one and the same. So the next time he pats your bottom in the kitchen or approaches you to make love when you fall into bed exhausted, instead of rolling your eyes or huffing a sigh, remind yourself that this is his expression of love for you. This is your husband turning to his bride to fulfill a deep emotional need that he has promised to look to no other for. Remind yourself what an awe-inspiring privilege it is to have this man look only to you for his deepest need.

If you want to go one further, don't wait for him to initiate! In today's culture, it often seems that for a Christian woman to openly express her sexual desire for her husband is viewed as inappropriate and indecent. Yet as we see at the end of verse 4 those who are with the Shulammite woman rejoice with her. They are celebrating her desire, her passion, and her fortune at marrying such a man. As wives, we must continually celebrate our joy, our fortune, and the desire we have in our husbands.

> **Think About it:**
> How do you think the Shulammite's open desire would be viewed by Christian sisters today? Do you openly show your husband that you desire him? Do you allow your breath to catch and your pulse to quicken in response to your husband like before your marriage, or have you allowed yourself to become distant towards sexuality in your relationship?
>
> **Take Action:**
> The Shulammite bride is boldly proclaiming how blessed she is to be marrying Solomon. Unfortunately, in our society today men are often viewed as bumbling idiots, and it is not unusual to hear a group of Christian women mocking their husbands or telling jokes about their many flaws. Sisters, you are your husband's mirror. If you view him as incompetent, he will view himself as incompetent. If you view him as overweight and worthless, he will view himself as overweight and worthless. Yet if he remains your knight in shining armor even in the hard times, he will view himself as capable and worthy. For the next week, seek out opportunities to openly praise your husband to others (especially if he can hear you!) and see how he reacts. (Caveat: the praise *must* be sincere!) Focus on your husband's unique talents, abilities, and strengths, and share those with the world!
>
> **Read Chapter 1:5-7**

Chapter 2 The Courtship   21

In this passage, we get a transparent look into who the Shulammite woman was as a person. It is likely that she grew up in the town of Shunem near Lebanon and that this is where Solomon found her (4:8) (Dillow 15). It is also possible that she was named after this town; however "Shulammite" can also be interpreted as the feminine form of "Solomon" (Dillow 15). This would mean that her very name describes her as Solomon's completion, his other half.

Despite this and having been carted off by her knight in shining armor (literally), plucked out of the fields where she was working and whisked away to the palace, she is still struggling with very real insecurities. First of all, she is insecure because of her dark skin. This is in no way a racial situation, but rather an economic one. She has been taken to the palace to become the king's wife, yet her dark skin marks her as a laborer. It appears that her father has died as she refers to her "mother's sons" making her work outside in the vineyard. In this day, ladies in the upper classes hardly did manual labor outside, so their skin would be much lighter in comparison. She is afraid that Solomon's court will judge her for having spent her life working in the vineyard.

She is also afraid of being unappealing to Solomon on their wedding night. She refers to working in the vineyard, while her own vineyard has gone unkempt. This means that due to her manual labor, she has not been able to care for herself physically as the ladies of the court would have done. Her beauty is completely natural, she has not had her hair or nails treated, she has not had expensive oils and perfumes, and she has not had expensive cosmetics. It is ironic that now she fears this will make her unappealing to Solomon, even though this is the exact state in which he found her.

There is some discrepancy when it comes to understanding verse 7. Some believe that this passage is indicating the Shulammite's insecurity and her fear of being able to please Solomon. She is afraid that while he is out in the fields he will be tempted by the prostitutes, and that she will have to dress/behave like a prostitute in order to compete and keep his attention (Petrillo 315). Others maintain that this is the Shulammite's concern regarding Solomon as king (Dillow 17). With his vast responsibilities, she is afraid that he will be inaccessible to her during the day. In short, this is her realization that to marry Solomon is to also marry his position. She may not be able to go to him any time she wishes, and this is something with which she will need to come to terms in order to marry him.

Think About it:
- In this passage the Shulammite is very open concerning her insecurities. What insecurities do you have as a wife?
- One of the Shulammite's insecurities seems to stem from the commonality of prostitutes, and her fear of being able to compete with them for her love's desire. This insecurity is very real for women today, especially those whose husbands are addicted to pornography. (There will be an entire appendix that will address overcoming pornography addiction.) In what ways is it unrealistic and unfair to compare ourselves and our sexuality to what the world throws at us in the form of underwear models, pornography, and the like?

Take Action:
Another one of the Shulammite woman's insecurities was tied to her husband's profession and his possible inaccessibility

during the day. Many women nag their husbands and give them tremendous grief over the hours they spend at work, rather than acknowledging their sacrifice to provide for their family. How can you be more supportive of your husband's efforts to provide for your family? What is something special you can do for him this week to show you appreciate him?

Read Chapter 1:8-11

Solomon's response to the Shulammite's doubt and fears is absolutely breathtaking. Rather than chastising her for her concern or ignoring her fears, he addresses them head on. He says that if she fears or has doubts about where he is or what he is doing, she can come to the fields and see for herself (Petrillo 316). He is reassuring her that his desire is for no other, and that he is willing to do whatever it takes to give her peace of mind.

Throughout our entire marriage, my husband and I have put safeguards in place for this exact issue. We share a Facebook account; we share an e-mail address. We have all of each other's passwords and are welcome to get on each other's devices at any time. Before one of us leaves, we tell the other where we are going and when we will be home. If plans change, we send a text or make a call to let the other know. I focus on our female friendships; he focuses on our male friendships. I don't spend time alone with another man, period, and he gives me the same respect in regard to other women. We have been mocked for this, disparaged, accused of not trusting each other, and labeled as "extremists." And you know what? All of that is just fine.

As we will discuss throughout this entire series, a successful marriage requires intentionality. Passive confidence that one would never be caught in an affair is simply not enough in our minds. We are intentional about protecting the sanctity of our marriage, whether others approve or not. This serves to protect not only our peace of mind, but our reputations. My husband is a minister, and we never have to fear allegations of inappropriate conduct being made against him. Why? Because he never allows himself to be in a position where it would have been possible. Allegations alone can destroy a man's reputation and family, whether there is any basis to them or not. Solomon is showing this type of transparency with his Shulammite bride. He is saying, "I only desire you, and here's the proof."

In this passage, Solomon lavishes his bride with compliments to assure her of his affection. While we may not appreciate being called a mare, for the Shulammite this would have portrayed unbridled desire (pun intended). In this era, it was common practice for the enemy to release a mare in heat among the stallions pulling Pharaoh's chariots (Petrillo 316). The ensuing chaos would give the enemy a distinct tactical advantage. Solomon is saying that she has the exact same effect on him. He tells her that she is lovely in her ornamentation. She has dressed up for him and he appreciates it. Then the chorus promises to lavish the poor, country girl with gold and jewels from her groom.

> **Think About It:**
> - Do you know what your husband's insecurities are? If so, have you responded to them like Solomon, or have you demeaned him for his struggles?
> - For many women, when we are engaged and our beloved

Chapter 2 The Courtship

compliments us as Solomon has the Shulammite, our eyes sparkle and our little hearts go pitter-patter. Years down the road, however, it can become hard to hear these compliments. Our husband says that we are beautiful, and our mind immediately goes to the pounds we have gained or our stretch marks from carrying his children. He says that you are wonderful, and all you can think of is that you got frustrated at the kids earlier and snapped at them. Do you find it hard to accept your husband's compliments and to believe them? If so, how can you work on that?

Take Action:
If you don't know what insecurities your husband struggles with, make time this week to ask him about them. Find out how you can help him be more confident in who he is and in your love for him. How safe is your marriage from outside influences? Is there need for greater transparency in your relationship? If so, what steps can you take to provide greater security and transparency in your marriage?

Read Chapter 1:12-14

While most English translations have the word *couch* in verse 12, a better translation is actually "round table" (Strong's #H4524). The imagery created here is of the Shulammite woman entering Solomon's court for a formal dinner. By comparing Solomon to myrrh, she is comparing him to one of the most valuable fragrances of the day. Myrrh was frequently worn by young ladies entering the presence of a king (Esther 2:12); they would sleep with it in a satchel between their breasts, and the scent would linger on them throughout the next day (Petrillo 318). She is telling Solomon that he is a beautiful fragrance that is constantly with her.

She also compares Solomon to henna blossoms from Engedi, which is an oasis that still exists today beside the Dead Sea. It is a beautiful, floral oasis with flowing water in the middle of the dry, dusty desert. The Shulammite is comparing Solomon to the beauty, peace, and life that is found in the oasis of Engedi, one of the most beautiful locations she would have known.

> **Think About It:**
> Throughout the text, Solomon and his Shulammite bride have both taken pains to include all five senses in the verbal banter leading up to their wedding. They mention the touch and taste of kisses, the rich fragrances, the visual beauty, and the sound of verbal affirmations. How many senses do you and your husband include in your relationship?
>
> **Take Action**
> Pick an evening this week to focus on remembering what making love was like early in your marriage. If you have kids at home, have them stay with friends or family or put them to bed early. Spend the evening focusing on how much you love this man you have shared so much with, and then show him! See how creative you can be in incorporating all five senses into your time together.

Chapter 3
Love's Consummation

As we approach this passage, we will see a definitive shift in the setting surrounding Solomon and his Shulammite bride. It appears that they have left their wedding feast and are moving to the bedchamber Solomon has constructed for her (Dillow 26). Throughout this section Solomon shares with us a delicate, tasteful, yet sensual description of the love and intimacy they shared on their wedding night.

Before You Begin:
As we approach the depths of the text and the intimate descriptions of Solomon and the Shulammite's lovemaking, take note of how you feel. Do you feel trepidation about Scripture's description of marital intimacy? Even though it comes straight from Scripture, do you struggle with feeling this is inappropriate? Are you excited to gain Scriptural guidance into fully enjoying your sexual relationship with your husband?

> **Take Action:**
> - Before beginning this study, pray for an open mind and an open heart. Pray that you will be able to take the beautiful picture of marital intimacy God has given us in this text and apply it to strengthening your own marriage.
>
> **Read Chapter 1:15**

Solomon is "setting the mood" by gazing into his beloved's eyes and telling her how beautiful she is to him. There are many suppositions as to exactly why he chooses to compare her eyes to doves; however of primary importance is the fact that, regardless of his exact reasoning, it is a statement of deep appreciation for who she is not just physically but also as a person. Remember, the eyes are the window to the soul. By comparing her eyes to doves, he is speaking to her beauty, her purity, and her innocence.

> **Read Chapter 1:16-2:1**

After this glowing statement from Solomon, the Shulammite woman responds in kind. While women today might shy away from telling their husbands that they are "beautiful," the fact remains that words of affirmation are just as important to our husbands as they are to Solomon. According to Gary Chapman in his best-selling book *The Five Love Languages*, words of affirmation are a primary love language for many of us (39). This means that if one of your husband's primary love languages is words of affirmation, this is something you need to be particularly attentive to. In addition, if one of your primary love languages is words of affirmation, this is something your husband needs to be aware of so he can effectively meet your needs in this area.

Next the Shulammite describes their surroundings. From the context, it is likely that they have arrived at their bedchamber. At this time in history, it was customary for the groom to build a special room for his bride as a wedding gift (Dillow 26). This is a special room just for her, and he takes great pains to ensure she would be comfortable there and that it would remind her of her country home. While it may not be realistic to ask our husbands to build us a special room, we need to take note of this special effort. Oftentimes, particularly after we become parents, our bedroom becomes a free-for-all. There are kids in and out, laundry piled up, and toys scattered throughout our bedroom.

It is hard enough to find time for intimacy as parents, and it becomes even harder if we don't have a secluded place to find solace and peace with each other. My husband and I were given this piece of wisdom years ago, and we have taken it to heart. We have a strict "no-kids-in-our-room" policy. Even though one of our only two bathrooms is in our bedroom, our kiddos know that they are not allowed in our bedroom without specific permission, period. They are certainly not allowed in our room without knocking, and they are not allowed to sleep with us. (When we had babies, they did sleep in a bassinet in our bedroom until they were about six months old.)

In addition, while our children have the run of most of our house, as evidenced by toys, art, etc. on display everywhere, our bedroom is off-limits. While I love my children with all my heart, there are no pictures of them or their artwork in our bedroom. Our room is decorated in colors that my husband and I find peaceful and romantic, I do my best to keep it picked up even if the rest of the house is disheveled, and the only pictures on the wall are of the two of us. It is our sanctuary. Our place of peace. The only place in our entire home that is set aside just for the two of us, and that has made all the difference.

> **Think About It:**
> How important are words of affirmation to you? To your husband? Is this something that you have spoken about with each other?
>
> **Take Action:**
> How romantic is your bedroom? Is it a place of peace? How can you make your bedroom a place of solace, and a place that encourages physical and emotional intimacy and peace?

At this point, we once again see the Shulammite woman's insecurity and humility. While in the church we have made "the rose of Sharon" a phrase we correlate with beauty and being set apart, this is actually the exact opposite of her meaning. While Solomon has been praising her beauty, she is saying that she views herself as plain, nothing extraordinary. In fact, the Septuagint actually uses a generic word for "flower" instead of "rose," in this passage, meaning they understood the Shulammite to be comparing herself to an average wildflower (Petrillo 326). This is further evidenced by her next statement--"a lily of the valley." She is saying that she is just one lily in a field of lilies.

> **Read Chapter 2:2**

Solomon responds to her statement by reassuring her once again that his affection is only for her. His response is beautifully empathetic to her insecurities. He points out that if she views herself as a simple lily, then all the other young women are thorns by comparison. I believe this is where many husbands and wives unintentionally strike a painful blow to their marriage. If Solomon had responded by saying, "Well sure, those other girls, they're pretty, but you're prettier." Would it have had the same effect on his bride? I have often heard husbands and wives both hurt their spouses when they make an "innocent" comment on the attractiveness of someone else. Sisters, we need to be very careful with our words. References to muscles, attractiveness, handsomeness, etc. should be reserved for our husbands, and yes, that includes the way we talk about TV stars!

Read Chapter 2:3-6

This is apparently the reassurance the Shulammite needed, as now we see the consummation of the love and passion between them. She is giving us an intimate description of making love with her groom. In this day "apple" and "apple tree" were frequently used as idioms to describe the physical, sexual act (Dillow 31). She is "in his shadow" as they make love, and she is praising Solomon for his sexual prowess. He is bringing her pleasure, and she wants him to know the pleasure and passion she feels for him.

The specific statement "his fruit was sweet to my taste" can have a variety of interpretations. One interpretation is that she is referring to the overall experience of making love to her husband; another is that she is referring to the literal taste of his skin and his kisses

(Dillow 31). Another possibility, however, is that this is a delicate reference to the oral stimulation of his genitals. Within ancient literature, "fruit" was often used as an idiom for a man's semen and genitals (Dillow 31). Regardless of the specific interpretation, it is clear that the Shulammite is fully engaged mentally, emotionally, and physically in making love to her husband. She is finding tremendous pleasure in him, and she wants him to know it.

> **Think About It:**
> Do you find it easy to verbally affirm your husband while making love? If not, why and how can you work to improve in this area?

Verse 4 is frequently misused and misunderstood. When she refers to Solomon's banqueting house, keeping it in context she is referring to their wedding banquet, the moment she becomes his, and he becomes hers. "His banner over me was love." This statement is beautiful. Keep in mind that her brothers made her do hard, physical labor. Yet under the banner of Solomon's house she now knows peace and protection like never before.

In verse 5, she is asking to be sustained, to be filled. Once again raisins and apples were frequently used when describing sexual love, and she is using this as a description of her physical desire for her husband. When she says that she is "sick with love," the literal meaning is deeply sexually aroused (Dillow 32). She is urging her husband to sate her desire for him.

Then in verse 6, she tells Solomon exactly how she wants him to fulfill her desires. She wants him to hold her close and to caress her. "Embrace" here literally means to stimulate sexually (Dillow 32). She is consumed with sexual passion and desire for her husband, and she is asking him to fulfill this burning desire within her. This is an intimate glimpse into a side of sexuality that is not openly discussed in the church today. She yearns to make love with her groom, and she has no insecurity in telling him so. Her desire is described in beautiful, fiercely intimate terms. She feels safe, loved, and cherished with Solomon; so much so that she is able to be completely raw and vulnerable with him regarding her sexual needs.

> **Think About it:**
> Are you able/willing to be so open and vulnerable with your husband sexually? Are you able/willing to lovingly tell your husband how he can best meet your sexual needs and what brings you the most pleasure as the Shulammite did for Solomon?
>
> **Take Action:**
> Set aside time this week for a special time of intimacy with your husband. Do your best to make sure you are well-rested and there are no distractions, so that you can fully engage mentally, emotionally, and physically in this time with him. Go slow and take the time to share with each other what you enjoy the most, and what brings you the most pleasure.
>
> **Read Chapter 2:7**

This verse is so important to teach our daughters. For the first time the Shulammite woman has engaged in sexual intimacy. We can tell from her description that this experience rocked her, changed her to her core. She has never before experienced such passion and desire. She now understands how special, how wonderful, God designed married love to be. With this understanding, she is now urging the young maidens not to awaken love before it pleases. She is pleading with them to not put themselves in situations where their lust, their passion, will be ignited until they can share that love with their husbands.

> **Think About it:**
> How does verse 7 apply to young women today? Is this something that is effectively taught in our homes and churches? Teaching young women to remain sexually pure is simply not enough. The truth is that for most individuals their sexuality is closely tied to their emotions. How will teaching young women to guard their hearts help prevent them from "awakening love before it pleases?" How can we do a better job of teaching our young women to guard their hearts? Do we inadvertently make it harder for young women to guard their hearts, and therefore their purity, when we ask questions such as, "Do you have a boyfriend?" Do we inadvertently put pressure on our single sisters, and thereby tempt them to awaken love, by treating them as though they are not whole until they are married?

Chapter 4
The Getaway

> **Before You Begin:**
> This passage gives us great insight as to how Solomon and his Shulammite bride make time to focus on each other. Think of the last time you and your husband set aside specific time for each other. In what ways did your marriage benefit from this time? If you don't remember the last time you did this, what barriers are preventing you from making time for each other? How can those barriers be overcome?
>
> **Read Chapter 2:8-9**

As this passage begins, we are given the impression that Shulammite is jolted from what she's doing by the long-anticipated sound of her lover's voice.

For Your Consideration:

In our age of technology, do we take the sound of our husband's voices for granted? Do we allow ourselves to still feel tingly when we hear their voices? Do our hearts lift and flutter when they call/text us during the day, or does it fill us with dread and the fear of another confrontation? Our answers and reactions to these questions give us an indication of where our relationships with our husbands are.

The truth is, we are only one half of our marriages. We have no control over our husbands and the way they interact/speak to us; however, we have total control over how we speak to them, and this speaks volumes about how we see our relationship. What does the majority of our communication with our husbands look like? Are we negative and nagging? Does it reflect what God wants for our marriages? I want us to consider whether or not the way we speak to and about our husbands reflects God's desire for submission in the marriage relationship. Sisters, "going along" with our husbands' desires/decisions yet giving them the cold shoulder when we disagree is not submission. Endlessly nagging our husbands is not submission. Not only are these behaviors not submissive, but they are death to both emotional and physical intimacy in our relationships.

Ephesians 5:22 tells us that as wives, we are to submit to our husbands as we would to the Lord. I would never tell God Almighty, "Fine, I'll do what you say, but for the record I think it's dumb," and then proceed to ignore Him. Yet wives regularly behave in just this way with their husbands. Our husbands do not have divine wisdom beyond what is found in God's Word. They are humans; they will make mistakes. Yet our consistent love and support, even when a mistake is made, gives them beautiful freedom to consider us first and foremost in their decisions. When we fight for our way, we undermine them, God's plan, and even ourselves as we make it almost impossible for them to truly consider us in their decision making. As mothers we rarely respond well when our children are in our faces yelling, "Me! Me! Me!" Let's make sure we aren't behaving the same way in trying to get "our way" with our husbands.

A Side Note:

If you are seriously struggling in your marriage, if you truly do not feel loved or feel like you and your husband are not currently able to meet each other's physical/emotional needs, I strongly recommend seeking outside help. Either find an older couple in the congregation to turn to (ideally an elder and his wife) or a professional Christian therapist. That being said, the books *The 5 Love Languages* and *His Needs, Her Needs* can be excellent resources for such struggles.

In verse 9 it appears that Solomon has been away and is now coming back to his bride. She admires his strength and virility as she describes him "leaping" and "bounding" like a young stag. As wives, it can be easy to focus on our own faults, and in turn the faults of our husbands. A wise, older sister once said to me, "A husband will become what a wife tells him he is." If we tell our husbands that they are lazy and overweight, they will be lazy and overweight. Yet if we admire their strength, their ability to open jars when we cannot, their desire to protect us, they will seek out further opportunities to do just that.

This verse also has a playful connotation to it. It appears that when she describes him as "looking through the lattice" he is almost playing "peek-a-boo" with her (Petrillo 334). According to Dr. Willard F. Harley in his book *His Needs, Her Needs*, for most men recreational companionship is vitally important (89). They need us to be fun and playful with them. I know that as a woman, particularly if there are still children in the home, oftentimes the last thing we feel like doing is having "fun," simply because it requires too much energy! (Let's be real, by the end of the day anything that requires more energy than flopping into bed can seem like too much.) Yet having fun––being light-hearted––is so important!

> **Take Action:**
> What can you do to have fun with your husband this week? What does he enjoy?
>
> **Read Chapter 2:10-13**

In this section, Solomon is asking his bride to go away with him. They have been separated, winter is over, spring is in the air, and he wants her to take time to go away with him. He describes the beauty that surrounds them, and then reminds her that to him, she is beautiful as well. It is wonderful to note that here, she is quoting Solomon. She remembers exactly what he said. His words were precious to her, and she committed them to heart (Dillow 45).

> **Think About It:**
> When your husband asks for your time and attention, do you happily agree, or is it hard for you? Do you feel that with the children, chores, outside job, etc., you simply cannot make the time? The truth is, after so many times of being rebuffed, our husbands will eventually quit asking.
>
> **Read Chapter 2:14-15**

There is some discrepancy regarding the interpretation of "clefts of the rock" in this section. Some maintain that he is literally referring to a mountain getaway. This fits with our knowledge of the Shulammite woman's home area; he is taking her away to a place where she will be familiar and comfortable. Yet we find similar wording in verse 17 where it reads, "cleft mountains," and this rendering is frequently understood to be referencing the cleft of the Shulammite's breasts. With either understanding, it is clear that Solomon is asking his wife to go away with him, to find a place of peace and solitude where they can enjoy being together.

It is important to notice what all this encompasses in Solomon's mind: he is focused on her physical beauty (your face is lovely) yet he also wants conversation with her (let me hear your voice, your voice is sweet.) In order to fully experience physical intimacy, we must have emotional intimacy as well. We must communicate openly and honestly with our husbands: What are our likes? Our dislikes? What are we excited about? What are we scared or frustrated about? But we must also communicate during lovemaking if our goal is intimacy. What feels good? What doesn't? What do we admire about our husbands? Their bodies? The way they make us feel?

When we come to verse 15, there is once again a lot of discrepancy in regard to interpretation. Some maintain that "foxes" is merely a reference to frolicking and playing together, and some believe that it ties back to verse 7 and is another warning for the maidens to keep their vineyards pure from the "foxes" that would mar them. Still others believe that the Shulammite bride is concerned about possible problems in their marriage, and she is asking Solomon to get rid of the hindrances before problems occur. This possibility is particularly strong considering that chapter three begins with the Shulammite dreaming about her fears concerning Solomon and their relationship.

> **Read Chapter 2:16-17**

Here we find the beautiful phrase, "My beloved is mine, and I am his." In every way, and with every fiber of their being, she is his and he is hers. They are giving themselves completely to each other mentally, emotionally, and physically. She is not mentally checking off her to-do list while she is with him, and she is not thinking "fake it 'til you make it." She is fully engaging her heart, mind, and body in being with her husband, and he is doing the same for her. They have both referred to her as a "lily," and now she describes him as "grazing among the lilies." They are making love, and she asks him to stay with her, to enjoy her throughout the night, until the dawn breaks.

> **Think About It:**
> Do we truly give ourselves wholly to our husbands when we make love, or do we find ourselves distracted and holding back? Do we "condescend" to have sex even though there are other things we "should" be doing? Do we, even inadvertently, make our husbands feel like sex-craved maniacs for desiring to be with us, when clearly we have more important things to take care of? 1 Corinthians 7:5 says that we are not to deprive each other, except for a limited time to devote ourselves to prayer and fasting. God created our husbands with a wonderful need (yes, *need*)

Chapter 4 The Getaway 41

to be physically intimate with us. But that need is only met when we are fully engaged. They don't want us to "sacrifice our bodies to their need;" they want us to need them, to want them as well.

Take Action:

Plan a special night alone for you and your hubby. If money is an issue, get creative! Find family or friends to keep the kiddos if they are still at home, get some bubble bath, candles, etc. from the dollar store, and turn your own home into a romantic oasis from the outside world. Turn off your phones and focus on each other! Talk about each other's lives, do something *fun* together, and spend the evening enjoying each other emotionally and physically.

Chapter 5
The Dream

> **Before You Begin:**
> Have you ever awoken in the morning furious with your husband, found yourself being snippy with him as he stares at you completely perplexed, all because of something that happened in a dream you had the night before? What about waking up terrified, and reaching for his strong, comforting presence for the same reason? There is no doubt that dreams are powerful and can drastically influence our moods and emotions. Before beginning this study, consider some of your most powerful dreams: How did they affect you? How did you cope with the emotional residue from your dreams?

Song of Solomon chapter 3 is widely accepted as being highly symbolic, and most agree that at least the first five verses are a recollection of one of the Shulammite woman's more powerful dreams. However, that is where the agreement on chapter 3 ends. Due to the symbolic and poetic nature of the text, it is difficult to tell with any degree of certainty what is literal, what is a dream, and what is a memory. With that being said, as we dive into chapter 3, we will cover as much of the context as possible, but our focus will be on the truths conveyed in the text, regardless of the specific context in which it is happening.

> **Read Chapter 3:1-5**

In verse 1 some translations read, "On my bed by night," and some read, "Night by night, on my bed." While this is not a huge difference, the more accurate translation is "on my bed by night," which tells us that the Shulammite is in bed dreaming; however, there is no textual indication that this is a recurring dream. She is dreaming that Solomon is gone, and she cannot find him anywhere. This ties back to the fears and insecurities we have seen throughout the text regarding Solomon's availability to her and is likely one of the fears referenced by the "foxes" in chapter 2. Her worst fear is coming true: She needs him, she wants him, and he is nowhere to be found.

Verse 2 is one of the key indicators that what is currently transpiring is a dream. It is very unrealistic that a woman, the queen, would have been prowling the streets at night alone. Yet in her dream she is so desperate to find Solomon that she doesn't let anything hinder her. She states, "I will rise now." She is not going to delay in seeking her beloved. Verse 3 adds further evidence to this being a dream when the city guards allow her to pass without showing any concern for their missing king or the terrified queen.

Various scholars have differing viewpoints on verse 4; I wonder if perhaps she has not been startled from sleep by her troubling dream. Either way, at last she has found the one her soul loves. Whether in wake or sleep, she clings to him and does not want to let him go.

She whisks him away to her mother's house, to a place of comfort and safety.

> **Think About It:**
> What is the significance of the Shulammite going away with Solomon? How would this time away have affected her concerns and insecurities? How do you feel about the idea of time away, alone with your husband? Do you believe this is an important and vital aspect of marriage, or does it conflict with the responsibility you feel for others such as your children, job, or aging parents? Where is your place of safety? Where can you go to escape the daily grind, the toils and struggles that are inevitable in life, and reconnect with your husband? What are ways we can protect our time with our husbands from outside influences and stresses when we just cannot get away?

Verse 5 once again cautions against awakening love before it pleases. Yet in this context the warning takes on an entirely new dimension. The Shulammite bride has deep-seated fears and anxieties regarding her relationship with Solomon. These fears have real-life validity when one considers the realities of being married to the king. Nonetheless, despite the realities of her concerns, she knows how much she loves him and that he loves her. As we are about to see, she turns to the memory of their wedding, of that very commitment, to comfort her in her time of struggle.

Once physical intimacy enters into a relationship, the entire dynamic shifts. If a couple engages in sexual activity without the foundation of commitment found in marriage, they have nothing to fall back on when the powerful emotions, inevitable doubts, and fears come into play. Here the Shulammite woman is warning the daughters of Jerusalem not to awaken those emotions until a lifelong commitment has been made.

> **Think About It:**
> How would you explain the commitment of Biblical marriage to someone with the world's "disposable marriage" mentality? Many people today base their relationships, and even the stability of their marriage, on the feeling of being in love. When they no longer "feel" love for their spouse, that must mean that the marriage is over. Yet my husband and I frequently say that love is not an emotion—it's a decision. Do you agree or disagree? Why?
>
> **Read Chapter 3:6-11**

After her terrifying dream and cautioning the daughters of Jerusalem against awakening love before it pleases, the Shulammite bride remembers the day her own love was awoken. With the fear of losing Solomon fresh in her mind, she remembers why she has no reason to fear—she remembers the day they committed themselves to each other. We share with the Shulammite the wonder she felt when she saw Solomon coming to claim her, take her away, and make her his own.

This would truly have been a sight to behold. In this day, it was tradition for the groom to gather a large processional to parade out and gather his bride, and this was a procession fit for a king. Solomon's Shulammite bride describes the cloud of smoke that could be seen from afar created by the exquisite fragrances burning all around the litter. The reference to a merchant implies that some of these were rare fragrances that were not native to the area and would thus have been very expensive.

When we see the word *litter*, it is exactly what we would imagine––a large throne or couch, suspended by poles, covered in curtains, and carried on the shoulders of men. Verse 9 is the only place in Scripture where this exact Hebrew word is found (Petrillo 355). From the Shulammite woman's description, it is clear that Solomon spared no expense. She describes it as being made from the famous trees of Lebanon, covered in silver, gold, and purple, and decorated for the king by his loyal subjects.

It is also clear that Solomon took his safety, and that of his bride, very seriously. Verse 7 tells us that the litter was surrounded by 60 of the mighty men of Israel. If this was a tradition carried on from David, then the phrase "mighty men" should be understood very literally. 2 Samuel 23 tells us that David's mighty men were able to kill hundreds of men each, and one even killed the brother of Goliath (1 Chronicles 20:5)! There is no reason to think David's son would have surrounded himself with any less.

This section concludes with the Shulammite encouraging the daughters of Jerusalem to gaze upon her beloved in all his glory, to watch as his mother crowned him. In the Jewish culture, it was tradition for the mother to place a crown of flowers on her son at his wedding (Dillow 68).

Think About It:
Many people today bemoan the extravagance and expense associated with modern weddings. While there is definitely some legitimacy to this concern, think about the impact it made on the

Shulammite when she saw the effort Solomon had gone to for her. What are things your husband does that make you feel cherished and special? What are things you wish he would do? Consider the opposite also: in what ways do you show your husband how cherished he is, and what are things he would enjoy that you don't currently do on a regular basis? Make sure to ask—don't assume!

Take Action:

Take time this week to remember the commitment that you and your husband made before the Almighty God. If you are fortunate enough to have a video of your wedding, pull it out and watch it. If not, pull out your photo albums and scrapbooks. If you have children at home, share it with them. Remember the wonder and excitement of that day. Remember that you are your beloved's and he is yours.

Chapter 6
Remember the Wedding Night

> **Before You Begin:**
> Think back to one of the most intimate times you have had with your husband, not just physically, but emotionally as well. What made it so intimate? Why is it so memorable for you?

In the last lesson, we walked with the Shulammite woman as she awoke from a terrible dream and began consoling herself with memories of her wedding and the commitment she and Solomon made to each other. It is only natural that the memories of her wedding also triggered memories of their wedding night. In this lesson we will gain an intimate, personal look into Solomon and his Shulammite bride's wedding night. How she looked, how she felt, and how her husband responded to her. Solomon and the Shulammite are both openly raw and vulnerable as they begin to explore and enjoy each other sexually for the first time.

> **Read the Entire Passage: 4:1-16a**

Notice that this entire passage is a verbal dialogue. It is doubtful that Solomon and the Shulammite are simply sitting still and looking at each other during this time. Most likely, this is what we indelicately refer to as foreplay. They are touching and kissing each other, arousing each other sexually. Note how relaxed the environment is—there is no rush, they are both perfectly content to take their time. They are also maintaining eye contact, as much of what Solomon says is a detailed description of his bride's appearance.

> **Think About It:**
> Do you take your time when making love with your husband, or is it always a rush so you can move on to other things on your "to-do" list?

When making love to your husband, do you allow him to visually enjoy your body? This can be very difficult as we are always quick to see our own flaws. However, it is also vitally important. It is no secret that most men are highly visual in their sexual arousal. When your husband is gazing at you while making love, he is not noting your flaws. He is noting the wonder of the woman with which God has blessed him.

There is tremendous intimacy in maintaining eye contact while making love, more so than many women realize. The book *Every Man's Battle* goes into great (and very informative) detail on the connection between sexual arousal and visual stimuli for most men. The truth, however, is that this type of eye contact can also be very uncomfortable for us, particularly if we are struggling in our marriage or feel very insecure physically or sexually. Because of the intimacy it brings, eye contact can also bring a tremendous sense of vulnerability. In fact, some studies have demonstrated a direct link between sexual arousal and where a man's eyes are focused as he climaxes (Weiss 15). This means that if his eyes are locked on you as he climaxes, it creates a direct chemical link in his brain between you and his sexual desire. What a tremendous honor!

Take Action:
- The next time you make love with your husband, make a point of taking your time and maintaining eye contact as much as possible, taking special care to maintain eye contact through climax.
- If you are insecure with your physical appearance to the extent that it is impacting your lovemaking, my challenge to you is to do something about it! Dr. Willard F. Harley states in his book *His Needs, Her Needs* that an attractive spouse is one of the top five emotional needs for most men (119-120). Granted, what each man views as attractive is going to be different—but make the effort to be attractive for him. He is worth it!

When looking at this text, it seems odd that this was viewed as romantic when most of us would be very offended to be compared to goats, pomegranates, and towers. Yet for the Shulammite, Solomon is offering her the greatest compliments of his day, comparing her to the most beautiful things he had seen. In this next section, we will briefly breakdown Solomon's metaphors and what they would have meant to his bride. It's beautiful to note that Solomon begins with her eyes and works his way down her body, enjoying every physical aspect that made her who she was, enjoying the fact that she was now his.

Verse 1 —— Solomon compares her eyes to doves, which we have previously discussed were a symbol of innocence and purity. He then compares her hair to a flock of goats on a mountain slope. These goats were different than our modern American goats. They had long, wavy black hair (Petrillo 365). The sight of a mountain of goats with long, wavy black hair blowing in a gentle breeze would certainly have been lovely to behold.

Verse 2 —— Her teeth are compared to a flock of shorn ewes. This indicates that her teeth were lovely, white, and straight, and that she had no teeth missing. The Shulammite woman might have been a country girl forced to work outside, but she had taken pains with her personal hygiene and he has noticed her efforts and appreciates them.

Verse 3 —— Her lips are like a scarlet thread and her cheeks are like halves of a pomegranate. This is likely a reference to the Shulammite wearing cosmetics, which would not have been uncommon at the time (Petrillo 366).

Verse 4 —— Her neck is compared to a tower. There are multiple interpretations of this verse. Some maintain that she truly had a long, slender neck. However, others believe that this is more metaphorical than Solomon's other compliments. He is saying that she is lovely yet strong. Her neck, and therefore her head, is held high. She carries herself with strength and dignity and is strong enough to give him the emotional support that he needs. It is consistently understood that the shields are a reference to jewelry she is wearing (Dillow 75; Petrillo 366).

Verse 5 —— Her breasts are compared to two fawns. The meaning here is multifaceted. He is saying that her breasts are lovely and symmetrical, yet this verse also provides evidence that there is physical contact transpiring as Solomon admires her beauty. This particular type of gazelle was considered a delicacy at Solomon's table, something that he greatly enjoyed the taste of (Dillow 76).

Verse 6 –– This verse provides evidence that this was an entire evening dedicated to sexual intimacy. He longs to be with her all night, until the new day breaks.

Verse 7 –– Solomon sums up his admiration of her physical beauty by once again saying that she is all together beautiful. There is nothing about her that displeases him.

Verse 8 –– This is likely a reference to what we could call a honeymoon. He is asking her to go away with him, to leave their everyday stresses behind and go to where they can focus on each other and find peace.

Verse 9 –– She is gazing back at him, returning look for look. It is clear that her equal desire for him is shining through her eyes as she looks upon her husband. The use of the word *sister* here is quite misleading. When combined with the word *bride*, rather than it being a reference to the family relation of sister, it refers to the lifelong, enduring relationship between the two of them.

Verse 10 ––Their time together is becoming increasingly intimate, and he is expressing the pleasure she is bringing to him and his desire for her. The reference to her "oils" is referring to her arousal, and her body preparing for intercourse. As women, this is hard for us to understand. When all works as it should, as we become sexually aroused our bodies produce a natural lubricant that allows intercourse without discomfort. This is how God, in His infinite wisdom, created us. Yet for many of us we can't help but view this as gross or smelly. However, for Solomon, this evidence of her arousal excited him even more, and for most husbands it is the same way. We do not need to be ashamed of how God created us, and we certainly should not be insecure when it comes to our husbands enjoying how God created us for our mutual pleasure.

Verse 11 –– The Shulammite has been kissing Solomon as he has enjoyed her body, and he is enjoying the taste of her. It is also possible that there are two meanings here, and she has been verbally appreciating Solomon as well. Yet another reminder of the power of words of affirmation in sexual intimacy. The word *garments* here is unique in Scripture, and not the word typically found for clothing in Scripture (Petrillo 372-373). It is implied that she is wearing some type of lingerie that Solomon found highly attractive.

Verse 12 –– This is a direct reference to the fact that the Shulammite woman was a virgin on their wedding night. The imagery created by description of a locked garden is quite beautiful. In this day, gardens were walled, protected, and highly valued (Dillow 82), a place of beauty, refuge, and peace. He is saying that her body is a thing of beauty that has been protected and cared for, just for him, that he can now delight in as her husband.

Verses 13-15 –– All three of these verses center on Solomon's enjoyment of her arousal. Her body is fragrant and inviting, and ready for intercourse, which she confirms in the next verse.

Verse 16 –– The speaker shifts from Solomon to the Shulammite. We know this because he has been referring to her body as a garden, and she now begs him to come and blow upon her garden. It appears that she has a good understanding of the anatomy of sexual

Chapter 6 Remember the Wedding Night 55

intercourse, much more than I am afraid many young women do today. She is comparing him to the wind and asking that he allow his spices to flow into her garden. This is an intimate request for intercourse, and she is telling him that she wants to feel him climax inside of her.

> **Think About It:**
> Solomon and the Shulammite are very open, vulnerable, and verbal as they make love. Which of these do you find the most difficult and why? In reading this detailed, intimate description of Solomon and his bride's wedding night, did it bring out any sexual struggles or insecurities that you need to discuss with your husband? What can you do to create a more emotionally intimate environment when making love with your husband?
>
> **Take Action:**
> Take time this week to focus on verbal/visual intimacy with your husband. Whether or not sexual intimacy follows is irrelevant, take the time to focus on each other and verbally affirm each other physically and emotionally.

Chapter 7
The Honeymoon Is Over

> **Before You Begin:**
> Think about the most common conflicts in your marriage. How do discussions about these conflicts normally go? What can you do to help overcome these conflicts, and minimize their detrimental impact on your marriage?

When we ended the last section, the Shulammite woman was remembering the passion-filled night she became Solomon's wife. It's important to remember, however, that this memory was triggered by her fears and anxieties. From the beginning she has been concerned about Solomon's job and its impact on their marriage. She has also felt rather alone and isolated, like maybe she didn't really fit in his world. Now we will see the culmination of her doubts and fears. In the form of another dream, we will observe a firsthand account of what the joining of two lives is really like. Even in a fairy-tale story where a working-class girl is literally swept off her feet by the king and whisked away to his palace, life is not all butterflies and rainbows. People are imperfect, and relationships are messy. Yet there is beauty still, because through this personal account we can learn how to strengthen our own marriages and our relationships with our husbands.

> **Think About It:**
> - In my experience, it seems that many Christian families feel a need to present only their best to the brethren. It is uncommon to hear sisters in Christ openly and honestly discuss their struggles, and those who do so frequently are often labeled as "dramatic." How do you think we can do a better job of walking the balance between over-sharing personal information and learning from and encouraging our sisters in Christ?
> - Do you think that Christian families presenting themselves in a way that appears they don't have significant struggles is detrimental to evangelism? Why or why not?
>
> **Read Chapter 5:2-8**

As this passage opens, the Shulammite woman is in bed sleeping fitfully. She's asleep but her heart is awake--she's dreaming. In her dream, Solomon was not with her. Once again, this has been a common theme of her fears, even appearing in an earlier dream in chapter 3. She has had to go to bed alone, yet as she sleeps Solomon comes knocking on the bedroom door. It's logical to assume that he has been engaged in business, although the text does not specifically tell us why he was not with her.

In this region, particularly during the dry season, it was very common for the dew to be so thick overnight that it would soak through a person's clothes (Dillow 101), so as he approaches her room he is completely soaked through, to the point he is dripping wet. Yet he is unconcerned, as his sole focus is on his desire to be with his love. He calls out to her with several terms of endearment and asks her to open the door and let him come in to her.

The Shulammite, it seems, is experiencing a wide range of emotions. She loves her husband, yet she's already in bed. She's tired, she doesn't have her clothes on, she's already washed her feet, and she simply does not feel like putting out the effort to be with him. Additionally, when one considers the entire context, I don't think it is extreme to assume she's also thinking, at least to some degree, "I knew this would happen! He had this coming! He wasn't available when I needed him, but now he expects me to jump up the minute he wants to have sex!"

> **Think About It:**
> Have there been times in your marriage that you felt all your husband was interested in was sex? How did you handle the situation? How could you have handled the situation better? Have there been times in your marriage that you felt your husband didn't "deserve" sex?

The Shulammite woman's reaction is the equivalent to a modern woman saying, "I have a headache," or even simply being so tired that it's not worth the energy to be intimate with her husband by the end of the day. There are jokes galore about this exact situation, but I strongly caution my Christian sisters that this is no joking matter.

I believe it is safe to say that the majority of marriages have a "desire differential." Frequently the husband has a substantially stronger sex drive than the wife, although it is not uncommon for the wife to have a stronger sex drive than the husband. There are also some relationships that flip-flop depending on what stress each spouse is under at the time. This is something that we must be aware of and prepare to be proactive.

Regardless of whether we are male or female, newlyweds or married 30 years, there is a distinct level of vulnerability when we make our desire for sexual intimacy known to our spouses. God created us with a sex drive, and He created the covenant of marriage as the means to fulfilling that sex drive. When we marry, we promise to fulfill this deep, emotional need for our spouses, and they promise to not have that need met anywhere else. Dr. Willard F. Harley's book *His Needs, Her Needs* does an exceptional job of explaining that our sex drive is an emotional need, not simply a selfish desire (50). As a need, it is cruel to deny our spouses such a vital part of marriage.

Whether we like to admit it or not, it is also unbiblical. First Corinthians 7:1-5 makes it clear that we are not to abstain from sexual relations in our marriages insomuch as we are able to be intimate with each other. As the mother of four children, a minister's wife, and a marriage and family therapist, I completely understand the total exhaustion that accompanies all the hats we wear as women. But at the same time, there is nothing so precious as a strong, capable, godly man entrusting you with his deepest, most vulnerable need.

Many years ago, a wise sister gave me this counsel, "Be careful with your no's." What she meant was that there are absolutely times when we are completely exhausted and just do not have the energy for sexual intimacy. There are times that we are sick, emotionally hurting, stressed, etc., and we simply have nothing left to give.

However, we need to be very cautious about rejecting our husbands' sexual advances (and truly, the same applies to our husbands meeting our sexual needs!) Next time you are not at all "in the mood" and your husband approaches you for sexual intimacy, instead of saying "no," asking him to give you 30 minutes or an hour. Believe me, by the time things are said and done, he won't mind! Remember that our brains are our most powerful sexual organ! Go take a bubble bath, fix your hair, put on lingerie, and think about being intimate with your husband. You will be amazed at what this will do for your desire for your husband! If you are truly sick, or just absolutely cannot be intimate for some reason, instead of saying "no," tell him that you love him and want to be able to fully enjoy being intimate with him, so what about tomorrow instead? Set a time: morning, evening, whatever works for you, and then *follow through!* It can be fun to have this time of intimacy for which to look forward!

For the busy moms out there—while it might not seem romantic at first, there is nothing wrong with scheduling sexual intimacy! Have a set day of the week where, regardless of anything else, you *will* be intimate with your husband! Once again, our brains are our most powerful sexual organ. Think about sex with your husband, send each other text messages and tease each other throughout the day, put him a little note in his lunch if he takes his lunch to work—the possibilities are endless! It's amazing how fun sex will be after an entire day of anticipation!

With all of this I have one more caution. Please, I beg you, do not ever "sacrifice" your body to your husband! I have known of wives who, when their husbands approached them for intimacy said, "Well, I don't want to, but fine." They might have had sex with their husbands, but there was no intimacy involved at all. That is not what he wants, and it will not meet his need! He wants you! He needs you! He needs to know that you need him as much as he needs you! If you simply "go through the motions," you are just proving that you do not desire him and he does not bring you pleasure. Take the extra time, put out the extra effort, and fully engage in making love with your husband

> **Think About It:**
> What are some ways you can increase both the intimacy and the frequency of making love with your husband? What are some ways you personally can use your thoughts to increase your desire for your husband? If you are in a relationship where your sex drive is stronger than your husband's, what are some ways you can work together to better ensure your needs are being met?
>
> **Take Action:**
> Schedule a time this week for sexual intimacy with your husband. Enjoy building each other's anticipation of this special time together.
>
> **Read Chapter 5:4-6**

Unfortunately for Solomon and the Shulammite, she did not have such advice, or if she did she didn't listen. In verse 4 Solomon goes so far as to reach through door to unlock the door himself, but he finally gives up and leaves about the time she realizes the pleasure she is passing up. She goes to the door to let him in, but she's too late. Her love is gone. There are two primary explanations for her hands dripping with myrrh, some scholars believe that Solomon had left his own scent on the door so that she would know he had been there, while others believe that the Shulammite had quickly applied her own scent to freshen up before opening the door for him (Petrillo 387; Dillow 102). Either way, the scent was pointless as Solomon had already left.

It's easy to blame the Shulammite woman for this relational boo-boo, and she was to blame for not being willing at first to put out the effort to be with her husband. But at the same time, this clearly transpired in the middle of the night, so Solomon's timing was terrible. As husbands and wives, we need to communicate openly and honestly about our schedules. Many people are truly and thoroughly exhausted by the end of the day, so bedtime is simply not a feasible time for intimacy. In your marriage early morning may work better, or right after work. Maybe, if work schedules are flexible, even lunch time works. There are endless options, but the important thing is to visit with your husband about what works best for your family at this time.

> **Think About It:**
> Do you and your husband need to do better planning regarding sexual intimacy? If so, how can you work on it?
>
> **Read Chapter 5:7-8**

The Shulammite was completely heartbroken when she realized what she had done. She called out for her love, but to no avail. She finally rushed out to the streets to search for him, and once again she comes upon the city watchmen. This time, however, they beat and abuse her. This seems to be indicative of her feelings of guilt for sending Solomon away. She knows she has hurt him, and she regrets it deeply. This section ends with the Shulammite woman begging the daughters of Jerusalem to help her find her love and tell him that she is sick with love. She realizes she made a mistake. Her own desire has now been aroused, but her love is nowhere to be found.

It is not uncommon for a "tit-for-tat" mentality to develop within a marriage. You hurt me; therefore, I will hurt you. You did not meet my needs; therefore, I will not meet your needs. Ephesians 5:22-31 gives a beautiful depiction of God's desire for the marriage relationship. It is important to note, however, that you will not find the word *if* anywhere in this passage. It does not tell wives to be submissive to their husbands *if* the husbands love them like Christ loved the church, or for husbands to love their wives as Christ loved the church *if* they are submissive to them. Rather, each spouse is accountable to God for his or her role in the marriage. God expects us to be loving, submissive wives, regardless of whether our husbands fulfill their role or not. This is a difficult and painful truth, but a truth nonetheless. According to 1 Peter 3:1-2, this level of selfless love may be the very thing that wins an unbelieving husband's heart to the Lord.

> **Think About It:**
> For the Shulammite woman, she literally felt beaten up by her guilt. Do you struggle with guilt over past mistakes that are affecting your relationship with your husband? How can you handle this guilt in a godly way? Have you been guilty of "cold-shouldering" or "punishing" your husband when upset with him? How can you work to change this pattern of behavior?

Chapter 7 The Honeymoon Is Over   65

Take Action:

This week, have an open and honest conversation with your husband about the emotional needs of both of you. What areas are you each doing well in? What areas do you each need to work on? *His Needs, Her Needs* by Dr. Willard F. Harley is an excellent resource for this discussion!

Chapter 8
A Different Perspective

> **Before You Begin:**
> Think about times in the past when you have had conflict with your husband. How do you each typically handle the situation? Do your typical reactions lead to a quick reconciliation, or do they cause a longer period of blaming/frustration before the situation can be resolved?

When we last left the Shulammite woman, she and Solomon had both made some mistakes that impacted their marriage. He had apparently been busy, and then gone to her in the dead of the night for sexual intimacy. This was very bad timing on his part, as well as very inconsiderate of her needs at the time. She, naturally, realized all of this, and ignored him when he came knocking on her door in the middle of the night. This in return left him feeling rejected and unimportant, so he left. And thus, we have a tremendous example of the cycle of dysfunction. A mistake by one spouse leads to hurt in the other spouse, causing him or her to react out of hurt and send hurt back to the first spouse, and if we aren't careful it can go on and on.

As we will see, through the medium of the "chorus," the Shulammite woman is given the opportunity to stop this dysfunctional pattern in its tracks. She's given the opportunity to choose a different perspective and a different approach to her heartache--a perspective which, as we will see, has the power to shift her entire focus and guide her towards reconciliation with her husband.

> **Read Chapter 5:9**

With a gentle prompt, the chorus is able to shift the Shulammite woman's focus from her hurt and frustration to all of the reasons she married Solomon in the first place. They simply ask, "What makes him so special?" Despite her current fear and pain, the Shulammite woman is able to immediately answer their question. This tells us that she regularly focuses on Solomon's positive attributes. She doesn't hesitate, she doesn't have to stop and think--she can immediately tell them why she is the luckiest woman in the world.

> **Think About It:**
> Where is your focus in regard to your husband? If you were asked what sets your husband apart, what makes you the luckiest woman in the world, how quickly could you respond? Do you focus on those things, or do you tend to focus more on when he leaves the toilet seat up or his dirty socks in the floor? Many times in relationships, we see what we look for. What do you look for in your husband?

> **Read Chapter 5:10-16**

This entire pericope is the Shulammite praising her husband. She praises his physical attractiveness, but as we will note she goes beyond that––she praises the way he treats her and the beauty of the relationship they have with each other.

> **Think About It:**
> - Imagine Solomon's reaction when he hears how his wife lovingly describes him. It makes me think of Proverbs 31:23: He is known because of her good deeds and kindness. He is respected because of his wife and her behavior towards him. Is this how your husband would feel if he heard how you talk about him to others?
> - In our society a lot of focus is placed on women's insecurities, particularly in regard to their physical appearance. It's important to remember, however, that many men struggle with their self-image as well (even if they won't say so because it isn't "manly"). How often do you praise your husband's physical appearance? Do you tell him that he looks handsome before he leaves for work? Do you verbally admire his body when you are being intimate?

Just as Solomon did for the Shulammite in chapter 4, the Shulammite begins with Solomon's head and works her way down his body, describing him and his attractiveness in detail. It appears that Solomon has inherited his father's looks, because she describes him as "ruddy," which is how David was described in 1 Samuel 16:12. She says that he is "radiant"––this could be a reference to his physical appearance, but it could also be a reference to his overall demeanor: he is confident and joyful. She describes him as being outstanding among 10,000 men.

> **Think About It:**
> Many women are good about complimenting their husbands, yet they also do not think twice about commenting on the attractiveness of actors in movies, etc. Can a husband view himself as, "1 in 10,000" when his wife is also commenting on the attractiveness of other men, even if that other man is one whom she will never meet in person?

In verse 11 she lovingly describes his curly, dark hair. There are multiple ways of understanding "his head is the finest gold." Some believe that this is a reference to Solomon having golden, tanned skin. However, it is also possible that she is describing his worth to her, his head––who he is as a person––is worth as much as the finest gold (Petrillo 392).

When we reach verse 12, she describes his eyes in the same way he described hers, by comparing them to doves. She goes a step further then and describes them as being beside a stream of water bathed in milk. She is saying that his eyes are pure and clear (Petrillo 392). His eyes are pure because only has eyes for her, and she knows it. He cares for himself, so his eyes are clear and not bloodshot from stress or a lack of rest.

Verse 13 describes his cheeks: however, she is likely referencing his beard. Regardless, it is clear that his scent, likely resulting from perfuming himself with spices, is appealing to her (Petrillo 393). She also describes his lips like lilies dripping liquid myrrh. When she compares his lips to the lilies, she appears to be complimenting their appearance. They are lovely and well-shaped (Petrillo 393). However, when she says that they are dripping myrrh, this is a reference to the fact that he does not have bad breath (Petrillo 393).

Think About It:

Throughout this study we have repeatedly seen the efforts that both Solomon and the Shulammite have gone to in order to be desirable to each other. They have both consistently perfumed themselves, worn nice clothes and jewelry, the Shulammite went to the trouble of applying cosmetics for him, and here we see him ensuring that he does not have bad breath. Personal hygiene is of vital importance in our marriages. Who wants to be intimate with someone who has bad breath and hasn't showered? Also, ladies, we need to make sure our husbands know they are worth some effort! Not all men like their wives to wear makeup, but we can at least put forth the effort to put on real clothes, make sure we smell nice, and fix our hair. Especially when we have little ones at home constantly grabbing at us, spitting up on us, etc., it can be very difficult to feel attractive. It can also be difficult to put out one more iota of effort because we already feel so drained! But it's important to remember, our husbands will be around long after our children have flown the nest. If we don't make sure they feel worthy of our time and effort now, they won't be interested in our "leftovers" then.

Take Action:

Sometime this week, surprise your husband by putting out extra effort. Take pains with your physical appearance, wear a perfume that he likes, and let him know it's just because he's worth it.

> **Read Chapter 5:14-15**

We now come to a more intimate description of Solomon's physical characteristics. His arms are rods of gold; they are strong and precious to her. His body is polished ivory bedecked with sapphires—it's smooth and strong, and the sapphires are likely a reference to jewelry he is wearing. His legs are compared to alabaster columns set on bases of gold. The word *columns* here is the same word used for the two great columns of the king's palace in 1 Kings 7:15-22, as well as the word for the cedars used in the litter which bore Solomon to her on their wedding day (Petrillo 394). His overall appearance reminds her of Lebanon, her home: a place of strength, safety, and comfort.

Verse 16 is truly beautiful, "His mouth is most sweet, and he is altogether desirable. This is my beloved and this is my friend, O daughters of Jerusalem." Scholars agree that the reference to his mouth here is not a reference to his kisses, but rather to the words that come forth from his mouth. He makes her feel special, he praises her, he tells her that she is cherished and adored, and she acknowledges how special that is. He is "altogether desirable," he is an amazing man inside and out, there is nothing about him she would change, and he is all hers! He is her beloved, and he is her friend.

> **Think About It:**
> Ladies, as we progress throughout our marriages, are we putting forth the effort to maintain our friendship with our husbands? The word for *friendship* here means companionship, loyalty, commitment and trust (Petrillo 395). Do we have companionship

> with our husbands? Do we make time to play with each other and simply enjoy each other's company? Are we loyal to him in every way? In how we speak, in our thoughts, and certainly in our hearts? Are we fully committed to our marriage in every way, and do we make sure everyone around us knows it?

The Shulammite concludes by saying, "This is my beloved, and this is my friend, O daughters of Jerusalem." She is saying, "You asked, well here you go." Teens today would likely say, "Boom!" or "Mic drop!" She's saying that's it, there is no more. He is wonderful, he is glorious, he is mine in every way--so take that!

Notice the amazing transformation of perception that the Shulammite has gone through in this passage: In the beginning she was hurt and frustrated, likely feeling both used and rejected. But now, she is in awe of her husband, and she feels blessed and privileged that he is hers and she is his! What changed? Not the circumstance. Certainly not the man. All that changed was her perception of the situation. She chose to focus on how blessed she is, and what a wonderful ~~man~~ God she was given by God. She switched her focus from herself to her husband.

Please don't misunderstand me--there are times when we have serious struggles in our marriages that need to be dealt with and addressed. There are times when we need to swallow our pride and seek outside help from a trusted older couple or a professional counselor. That being said, there are also times when we are simply selfish. When we are focused on what we want, what we need, how we feel, and we lose sight of the fact that there is another human in this relationship who also has needs, struggles, and feelings.

These are the times that little things can easily become blown out of proportion and wreak havoc on our relationship. This is when it would behoove us, and our marriage, to take a breath and take a step back. To intentionally switch our perception from our hurts and frustrations to the blessings we have in our husbands.

> **Take Action:**
> Take time to sit down this week and focus on all of the things your husband does right. Make a list of the ways he shows you he cares for you and the ways he serves your family. For instance, just this morning I received a text from a dear friend. It simply said, "This means 'I love you,'" and it was a text from her husband where he had changed the oil in her vehicle for her before she traveled. Because our husbands are *not* women, they will not always communicate their love to us the way we would, or the way we want them to, but that doesn't mean they aren't communicating. Look for the ways he is showing you and be thankful.

Chapter 9
Together Again

Before You Begin:
Think about a time when you and your husband have had a falling out. What was the reconciliation like? Was it all at once, or was there some residual hurt and frustration for a while? Were you able to give and receive an apology and move on, or did one of you feel that more needed to be done before your relationship could get fully back on track?

In our last lesson, the daughters of Jerusalem (or chorus) helped the Shulammite woman re-direct her thoughts. Rather than focusing on her hurt, fear, and frustration, they guided her towards focusing on how desirable her husband is. This change in perception helped the Shulammite woman overcome her doubts, fears, and hurts, and be ready to reconcile with her love.

Read Chapter 6:1-3

The Shulammite's detailed description of her husband has definitely sparked the interest of the other women. They basically respond by flattering her and saying, "Pretty lady, we will help you find your beloved!" The implication is that after such a description, they want a glimpse of this amazing man!

The Shulammite woman's response is priceless. She basically says, "Yes! Be jealous! He is all mine!" (Garrett 415). She uses the same metaphorical language we have seen throughout the text to tell them in no uncertain terms that she is his, and he is hers, in every possible sense (Garrett 415). While we all know that jealousy in sinful, a certain amount of possessiveness when it comes to our husbands is not a bad thing. We should be proud of "our men," and there is wrong with letting others know when the occasion calls for it. I have actually heard women begin to point out their husbands' flaws when they are complimented by other women. There is nothing wrong with saying, "Yes, he is wonderful; I'm so thankful God blessed me with him!"

> **Think About It:**
> Oftentimes as Christian women, we inadvertently communicate that we must downplay any compliments we receive in order to not be prideful. While we should certainly not go around bragging on ourselves, there is nothing wrong with saying, "Thank you, God has blessed me," when receiving a compliment. This should be the case with our husbands and children as well. When someone makes a comment about your husband doing something well, do you find yourself responding with a comment such as, "Yes, but he sure has a temper too!"?
>
> **Read Chapter 6:4-10**

Chapter 9 Together Again   77

With loving thoughts flowing through her mind, the Shulammite woman is finally reunited with her love. It seems as though Solomon is eager to reconcile with her and make up for his own part in their falling out. He immediately begins praising her, reaffirming his love and dedication to her. To help us understand the imagery he uses, we will break it down verse by verse.

Verse 4 –– Tirzah was an ancient city known for its beauty and gardens (Petrillo 404). The word *army* is not found in the Hebrew. The idea of this comparison seems to be that inspires the awe and majesty of many flowing royal banners (Petrillo 405).

Verse 5 –– Her eyes are so enticing that he feels he is being held captive in her gaze, such is her power over him. Also in this verse, we see the first of many repetitions of his earlier praise (4:1). The idea is that over time, now that he knows her as intimately as possible, she has not diminished in his eyes at all. His love for her is as strong now as on the day they were married (Garrett 416).

Verse 6-7 –– A repeat of 4:2-3.

Verse 8 –– Solomon's mention of queens, concubines and virgins (or maidens) should not be assumed to be a direct comparison. As with everything else in this context, Solomon is making a metaphorical comparison. He is saying that out of every queen, concubine, or maiden, she is the loveliest.

Verse 9 –– The reference to queens and concubines ties back to verse 8. Even those of royalty acknowledge her beauty. When she is described as the only one of her mother, we know that this is not a reference to her being an only child due to the mention of her brothers in 1:6. Solomon is simply stating that she is the favorite, beyond comparison.

Verse 10 — There is some disagreement regarding who is speaking in verse 10. Some maintain that it is still Solomon; however, it makes sense that this is the response of the daughters of Jerusalem. Much as they asked the Shulammite about her beloved, they are now asking Solomon, "Who is this glorious woman?" Solomon's response is a repeat of 6:4, and most likely has the same meaning (Petrillo 410).

> **Read Chapter 6:11-12**

Verse 12 is the single most debated verse in the entire book. However, we must remember that the Shulammite woman has had two primary struggles throughout the text: (1) Her fears about Solomon's job keeping him away from her, and (2) Her insecurities regarding leaving her home and fitting in at Solomon's royal court. When looking at the entire context of all that has happened, it appears that in verse 11 the Shulammite woman has stepped into an orchard to "catch her breath" from all that has happened. While she is in the orchard, she realizes that she must leave her old life behind, and "leave and cleave" (Genesis 2:24). Everything has happened very quickly for her, yet she realizes that it is time to take her place among Solomon's chariots and return home with him.

> **Think About It:**
> For the Shulammite woman, leaving and cleaving literally meant leaving behind everything and everyone she had ever known. She could not simply hop in the car and drive 20 minutes to see her family, she couldn't follow them on Facebook, and she certainly couldn't Facetime them in the evenings. Yet she has accepted that making her marriage work will mean focusing on her husband

first and foremost. What impact do you think modern technology has had on leaving and cleaving when we marry? How would you help a young bride understand the concept of biblically leaving and cleaving?

Take Action:

This week make the time to have an open and honest conversation with your husband regarding the idea of leaving and cleaving. Do you each feel you have done this appropriately? How do you feel about your current balance between caring for your parents and focusing on your marriage? Are there changes that need to be made?

Chapter 10
Solomon Delights in His Wife

Before You Begin:
Think about a time when you felt particularly torn between two decisions, or perhaps even between your husband and your family of origin. Did you feel that your husband was a source of strength and encouragement during this time? Were you able to have healthy, open, and honest communication, or do you believe this is an area you need to improve on in your marriage? Is your husband confident that he is your first priority, or does he feel that he has to compete with other people in your life?

As we left the Shulammite woman in our previous lesson, she had finally reached the point where she was able to release her reservations and focus wholly on being Solomon's wife. Throughout this next section, we will see Solomon's reaction, and the beauty of the newfound unity in their marriage.

Read Chapter 6:13

It is important to remember that the others, the daughters of Jerusalem, or chorus, whichever your translation may identify them as, are a literary tool. Once again, this is poetic literature, and these characters serve the purpose of guiding us through the various scenes as an observer. In the first part of verse 13, they appear to symbolize the emotional pressure the Shulammite felt upon leaving her home and fully embracing her life at the palace. They miss her, and they want to see her again. Yet her decision has been made. This doesn't change the fact that she loves those she has left behind; however, her focus must now be on her husband.

There is a tremendous amount of disagreement concerning the latter part of verse 13 and who is speaking. Some maintain that this is Solomon, and much as the Shulammite did earlier in chapter 6, he is saying, "Back off, she is mine! You have no right to gaze upon her!" With this interpretation, the "two armies" referenced are actually groups of individuals, and this is a public party (Petrillo 415). He is acknowledging that she stands out among all those present but also emphasizing that he is the only one who has the right to fully appreciate her beauty.

A second opinion is that the Shulammite woman herself is speaking here and is engaging in playful banter with Solomon. This interpretation maintains that Solomon and the Shulammite are now alone in the palace, and she is seductively dancing before him (Dillow 131). She knows how her dance is affecting him and she is enticing him, "Why would you stare at little ol' me?!"

Interestingly enough, in both the Hebrew and the Greek renditions of this text, verse 13 actually starts chapter 7 (Petrillo 412). It is unclear why our English translations have chosen to incorporate it into chapter 6; however, what is clear is that this prelude sets the stage for all that will occur in chapter 7. Additionally, the discrepancies among scholars concerning who is speaking verse 13 serve as a potent reminder: When it comes to our English translations, all subheadings are uninspired and added by men. Particularly within the Song of Songs, if we automatically assume the translators were correct every time they identify the speaker within a scene, we run the risk of misinterpreting what is being said, or at the very least approaching the text with an inaccurate preconceived idea.

It is also interesting to note that this is the first time the name "the Shulammite" has appeared in the text. There is a definite article in the Hebrew, so it truly reads, "the Shulammite" (Petrillo 413). By way of reminder there is also disagreement within scholarly realms concerning the meaning of *Shulammite*. The primary schools of thought are that: "Shulammite" is a reference to the city of Shunem, which was at this point called "Shulem" (Petrillo 413). According to this understanding, "the Shulammite" is simply a reference to where she is from, much as is seen in reference to "the Ethiopian eunuch" in Acts 8:27.

A second opinion concerning the identification of "the Shulammite" is that Shulammite is actually the feminine form of "Solomon" (Dillow 15). Those who maintain this belief state that the very identification of "the Shulammite" identifies her has Solomon's beloved, as the one who is in every sense of the word his other half. It is a beautiful identification which surely sent butterflies through her stomach, much as the identifiers of "wife" and "Mrs." should for us today.

> **Think About It:**
> There seems to be a growing trend in American society of women not taking their husbands' names or choosing to hyphenate their names rather than drop their maiden names completely. What are your thoughts concerning this? How does it apply to the Shulammite's identification as "the Shulammite?" Does it detract from our individuality, or is it a descriptor of a beautiful new identity in our marriage? Is it both?
>
> **Read Chapter 7:1-6**

In this section Solomon is once again glorying in his wife's body; however, this time he begins with her feet and travels to her hair. His descriptions in verse 1 add credence to the idea that she is dancing before him. However, because of the sensual nature of his description and the fact that some of his description would require little if any clothing, it is doubtful that anyone else is around. They are once again alone and enjoying each other.

He begins by describing her sandaled feet. This may seem odd, particularly if they are indeed being sensual in the bedroom; however, remember her comment from 5:3--at this time they did not typically remove their shoes until they were ready to wash their feet for bed in the evening. There is definitely an implication that being on the floor barefoot would have dirtied her feet in chapter 5, so it is logical to assume that the same would be true here (who wants dirty feet when making love?!)

He also compares her rounded thighs to a masterpiece. In the Hebrew, the more accurate translation is "curving hips" (Dillow 133). This is further evidence that she is dancing and swaying before him, allowing him to delight in her appearance. The reference to "noble" or "royal" daughter is very sweet and considerate of Solomon. He is aware of her struggles, her sacrifice, and her insecurities. He's telling her that she fits here, that she is right where she belongs (Petrillo 422).

Next, in verse 2, he describes her naval as being a rounded bowl never lacking wine, and her belly as a heap of wheat encircled with lilies. The word for *naval* here is difficult, as it only appears two other times in Scripture: Ezekiel 16:4 and Proverbs 3:8 (Petrillo 422-423). While the exact word provides some difficulties, many scholars agree that this is a reference to the female genitalia (Dillow 133-134; Petrillo 423). He is saying that in the most intimate ways, he never lacks for pleasure from her body. As Solomon is describing her from her feet up, and his next observation clearly does refer to her belly, this understanding is logical and fits with the text. There is also some ambiguity concerning the word *belly*. Some maintain that he is admiring her belly, others state that this is a reference to the fertility of her womb as a woman. Either way, by drawing comparisons to wine and wheat, Solomon is saying that her body is a delicious feast that he longs to enjoy (Dillow 134).

In verse 3 he once again compares her breasts to the twins of a gazelle (see 4:5). It is almost as if this is a passing thought as he moves his eyes along her body, however in verses 7-8 he will come back and dwell on the appeal and pleasure he finds in her breasts. This gives the impression that he is seeing the beauty and pleasure she has to offer as she moves before him, but as their loveplay progresses he will focus in the parts of her body he enjoys the most.

> **Think About It:**
> How would you feel if your husband were to verbally praise your body in detail as Solomon does? Would you believe him? Would it make you feel insecure, or loved and cherished? Are there changes you need to make in order to be comfortable with your husband enjoying your body?

With verse 4 Solomon once again compares her neck to a tower, implying that he views the Shulammite as regal, poised, and strong. She holds her head high, in spite of her struggles and insecurities, and is still ultimately able to be confident in who she is and his love for her. As sweet as this is, it is difficult to read the end of verse 4 without cringing just a little bit. Most of us would probably cry if our husbands, however lovingly, informed us that we had noses like a tower. However, in this day a prominent nose was seen as adding symmetry to facial features and as a mark of nobility (Petrillo 426).

> **Think About It:**
> In the church, we talk a great deal about humility and the evils of pride. Yet most men find a sense of self-awareness and self-confidence to be attractive. For instance, most men become frustrated when their wives belittle themselves or diminish their compliments. As Christian women, how can we better find the balance between being confident in who we are and whose we are and not being prideful?

In verse 5 Solomon describes her hair as a crown, once again gently reiterating her worth to be by his side. He is open and vulnerable in telling her the power she holds over him. In spite of all his strength and power as king, he is held captive by her beauty. He concludes his description by reminding her that she is altogether pleasant and brings him tremendous pleasure. He delights in her physically and emotionally. She gives him both peace and fulfillment.

> **Read Chapter 7:7-9a**

At this point, Solomon is very clear about how aroused he is, and exactly what is on his mind. He compares her to a palm tree, which was known to be tall and slender (Dillow 135). The direct imagery of intercourse here is unmistakable. In this day, it had long been a practice to artificially fertilize the date palm trees. Men would climb up the male trees and retrieve pollinated blossoms, tie them together, and then climb up the female tree to place the pollinated male blossoms among the female blooms (Dillow 136). She is lovely, she smells nice, and he longs to caress her body and taste of her. The word for *mouth* here actually means "palate" (Petrillo). He concludes his speech with a deep, passionate kiss.

> **Think About It:**
> Throughout the Song of Songs, there has been repeated mention of sight and smell in regard to sexual pleasure. It's interesting to note that these observations have been made by both Solomon and the Shulammite woman. It can be difficult to desire intimacy with someone who is unclean or does not smell good, it can be difficult to desire intimacy in an environment that does not smell good, and it can be difficult to desire intimacy with someone who has made no effort to be visually appealing. Where are you and your husband in these areas? Are these areas that you put forth

effort in, or does some improvement need to be made?

Read Chapter 7:9b-10

The speaker changes here, and the Shulammite woman begins to respond to Solomon. She tells him that their love is smooth, and their bodies will glide together. She knows that he desires her and rejoices in it. She is assuring him that she feels the same, and his desire will not go unfulfilled.

Think About It:
Do you and your husband rejoice in your sexual desire for each other, or has it come to feel more like a burden to be endured? How can you work to improve this area of your relationship?

Take Action:
Solomon concluded his speech to the Shulammite with a deep, passionate kiss. In the hustle and bustle of life, for many couples kissing in any form other than a peck on the cheek as one spouse darts at the door can become a long-forgotten memory. Over the next week, make a point of sharing a deep, passionate kiss with your husband at least once a day. Note any changes this creates in your relationship.

Chapter 11
A Romantic Rendezvous

Before You Begin:
When was the last time you and your husband went away, just the two of you? Is this something that you have made a consistent aspect of your marriage? Do you feel guilty going away with your husband if you still have children at home? .

Throughout this book we have seen Solomon and the Shulammite's love grow and blossom. We have seen them inadvertently push each other away and struggle with doubts and insecurities, and we have seen them come back together and work through their struggles. After all that they have been through, the Shulammite wisely determines that they need some time away. They need time without distractions to focus on each other and to reaffirm their love for each other.

Read Chapter 7:11-13

In verse 10 we know the Shulammite woman was speaking due

to the use of the personal pronoun "his." There is no indication of a change, so it is safe to assume that the Shulammite is still the speaker. She is boldly, plainly, inviting Solomon to go away with her for a romantic rendezvous. Not only that, but she makes her plans for this rendezvous known from the very beginning. She wants to whisk him away from his responsibilities and go out to the vineyards. It appears to be spring as she wants to see if the vineyards are in blossom, so it's possible that this could be around their anniversary (see 2:10-14) (Dillow 138).

Once they arrive, she intends to make love with Solomon in the fresh air, surrounded by the natural beauty of God's creation, while the mandrakes give their fragrance. If you remember back to Genesis 30:14-16 Leah "bought" time with Jacob by giving her son's mandrakes to Rachel. This clearly indicates that they were considered a sign of fertility, and it appears that the Shulammite woman considers their fragrance to be an aphrodisiac. Then, in a manner which would probably lead many of us to blush, she tells Solomon that she has all kinds of sexual treats in store for him. She says, "choice fruits, new and old, which I have laid up for my beloved." She has learned what brings Solomon immense pleasure, but she also has some new sexual delights she intends to experience with him.

There are many things that we as wives can learn from this passage. First of all, the Shulammite is the one who instigates a sexual retreat for her and her beloved. Ladies, you need to initiate lovemaking with your husband. He needs to know that you desire him, and that you want to please him sexually. And while yes, it's wonderful to plan special time at home, it's also important to get away. Leave the children, leave the stresses of work, and go somewhere just the two of you. I am not sure where it originated, but one of the greatest quotes I have ever heard is this: "The most loving thing parents can ever do for their children is to put their spouse first."

This was really driven home to me about six years ago, when our children were still in public school. Our oldest daughter was in about the fifth grade, and I could tell something was wrong the minute she got in the car after school. I asked her what had happened, and she began to cry. Not one, but two of her closest friends had told her that their parents were getting a divorce that day. She hurt for her friends, but she was also terrified. If it happened to her friends, didn't that mean it could happen to her also? This showed me just how important it is for our children to *see* that our marriage comes first. My husband and I have tried to make this a priority throughout our marriage, as much as time and money would allow, and have emphasized regular date nights, and at least one weekend a year for just the two of us.

The result? Our children plan date nights for us. It's the sweetest thing ever, and it completely blew us away the first time they did it. Every great once in a while they will get together and plan, and they set out candles, encourage us to dress up, cook supper for us, serve us, and then go to a bedroom to play games together for the evening. Why do they do this? Because they know that Mom and Dad come first, and that it takes time together to keep it that way. It gives them comfort, encouragement, and stability to see us being intentional about making time for our relationship. So mamas, if you feel guilty about leaving your littles behind for a weekend of frisky frolicking with your hubby––don't! Making time for your marriage is another vitally important way of showing your children how much you love them.

It's also important to note that the Shulammite was creative in planning this special time away. First of all, she had noted (and likely discussed with Solomon) what he enjoyed in their lovemaking and what brought him the most pleasure. She's being quite the wicked tease here as she says, "Oh yeah, that stuff you *really* like––it's coming!" However, she has also put thought and effort into coming up with new ways to experience their sexuality together. Sisters, sex is not just for procreation; God intended it to bring us great pleasure! It should not be boring and mechanical––it should be passionate and exciting!

Here's where I would like to offer some practical guidance and advice. I believe that here, God's Word is encouraging us to be creative in our lovemaking. This means that there is more than one God-approved means of having intercourse. Along these lines I offer two practical guidelines:

1. It is not okay to engage in any sexual activity, even with your husband, that violates one of your consciences or makes one of you feel uncomfortable. Our sexuality is a beautiful gift from God that He intends for us to embrace and enjoy within the marriage relationship. If one spouse is being pushed into doing something that violates his or her conscience or makes him or her uncomfortable, that beauty and safety is lost.

2. I advise not bringing anything into the sexual relationship that violates the sanctity and pleasure of the marriage relationship. For instance, study after study is showing the detrimental effects of pornography on marriage. Many couples, and indeed

many therapists in the past, have believed that this could be an effective tool for "spicing up" the sexual relationship. However now we are seeing just how detrimental this is to marriages. (Resources for these issues will be included in our final lesson.) Along these lines, there are various "toys" that can be purchased for the same reason. I strongly recommend caution in bringing anything into the sexual relationship that could potentially make your bodies less responsive to each other. If you purchase "toys" for stimulation, there is the risk of conditioning the human body to where it requires that "extra" stimulus in order to become aroused. This would mean that out of the good intention of "spicing up" your love life, you can actually inadvertently condition your bodies to where they no longer respond to simple human touch.

> **Think About It:**
> Have you ever planned a special weekend for you and your husband? How do you feel about the Shulammite woman's boldness and creativity in regard to their sexual relationship? Have you and your husband inadvertently brought things into your sexual relationship that could be detrimental to your intimacy? Is this something that needs to be talked about openly in your relationship?
>
> **Read Chapter 8:1-4**

Verse 1 seems very odd to us, as she is comparing her lover to a brother; however, we need to be careful not to read too much into this analogy. She's not saying that she literally wishes they were brother and sister, but rather she is saying that she wishes they had always been together (Petrillo 438). She wishes they had always been close enough that she could run into him outside and kiss him any time she wanted.

Verse 2 is demonstrating the beauty of maintaining good relationships with the in-laws. She wants to take him home to her mother, where she learned to be a wife. She wants him to be around her mother, to learn a deeper aspect of why she is who she is. This is also a beautiful example of Titus 2:3-5. She has learned how to love him, how to be a wife, from her mother.

> **Think About It:**
> - Not all women are blessed to be raised by Christian mothers. How can we fill the gap for these sisters, and better fulfill Titus 2:3-5?
>
> - When it comes to in-law relationships, balance is so important! We have discussed leaving and cleaving; however, Scripture also makes it clear that our parents deserve a certain level of respect and that we are to care for our parents as they age (1 Timothy 5:4). How does this balance look in your marriage? Is it something that you need to work on?

In the latter part of verse 2, the Shulammite woman further elaborates on what she would like to do with Solomon. The personal pronoun "my" indicates that she longs for him to "drink" of her body. This is further emphasized by verse 3, which is a direct quote from chapter 2:6.

Then in verse 4, we see the Shulammite's final plea to not awaken love until it pleases. She has now experienced the good times and the bad with her husband, and she is as convinced as ever that love should not be awakened until it is within the godly confines of marriage. Some versions include personal pronouns such as "my" and "she" in this verse, however these pronouns are not found in the original Hebrew text (Petrillo 440).

> **Read Chapter 8:5-7**

Solomon and the Shulammite woman are now returning from their getaway arm in arm. Their strife and worries have been left behind, and all is well with their relationship. After warning the daughters of Jerusalem to not awaken love until it pleases, she states that she has awakened the love of Solomon. In verse 2 we saw a reference to the Shulammite's mother, and now we see Solomon's mother mentioned. The Shulammite is acknowledging his home and his connection to his mother as well. This is a praise of the beautiful balance that God created sexual intimacy to be. It is not pure sexual desire. It is not only for pleasure. It is not only for procreation. Yet all of these things play a part. The Shulammite has cautioned against prematurely awakening sexual desire, she has exulted in the joys sexual intimacy have brought to her, and now she celebrates the multi-generational aspect of preserving the family line through sexual intimacy (Petrillo 442).

> **Think About It:**
> It is certainly true that Solomon and the Shulammite have just had a wonderful time of sexual passion, focusing on each other. Yet as they return, they do so with their arms casually linked together. There is an important balance between sexual touch and non-

> sexual touch demonstrated here. However, it's also important to remember that this balance will be different for every couple. Some couples feel great emotional intimacy by simply sitting together in a room, while others thrive off being in actual physical contact (whether holding hands, arms around each other, etc.) as much as possible. It is important to talk about this with your husband to find out what each other's specific needs are in this area. When you see public displays of affection from other couples, how does it affect you? If you are honest do you think, "Aw, look at that, how sweet!" Or do you think, "C'mon people, get a room!" Do you think the church encourages intimacy in this way or discourages it (specifically regarding married couples)?

Verses 6-7 are especially impactful when viewing the Song of Songs in its entirety. Throughout the book, there has been a tremendous emphasis on the sexual intimacy of marriage. However, verses 6-7 remind us that the marriage relationship is about so much more than sexual intimacy! The Shulammite woman wants Solomon to place her as a seal over his heart. This speaks to the deep level of emotional intimacy that is necessary in a Biblical marriage. Each spouse has fully entrusted his or her heart to the other. Your spouse sees the good, the bad, and the ugly in you, and, in the words of my mother, "loves you warts and all."

These verses also give an interesting insight into the concept of jealousy. There are only two relationships in all of Scripture where jealousy is acceptable: the divine-human relationship, and the marriage relationship (Petrillo 444). She is saying that with the intense love created by the intimacy of marriage also comes intense jealousy. Sisters, we need to jealously protect our marriages!

This means jealously protecting the sanctity of our marriages from outside relationships, and even the influence of media, etc. This means jealously protecting the intimacy of our marriages by guarding the heart our husbands have entrusted to us. This means jealously protecting the intimacy of our marriages by being emotionally safe ourselves. Can our husbands trust us with their hurts and struggles? Can we handle it without becoming emotionally unstable ourselves? Can we keep our mouths shut when they share with us? Can we handle their insecurities and struggles without belittling our husbands for them or using them against them later? This means jealousy protecting the unity of our marriages from our children. Do *not* let your children play you and your husband against each other!

My dear sisters, Satan is alive and well. He wants you, and he wants your husband. He wants your children, and he will do anything in his considerable power to get what he wants! We *must* be proactive in jealously protecting the families God has entrusted to us!

> **Think About It:**
> Do you and your husband jealously protect your marriage? Is this an area you need to work on together? If so, how can you do better at this?

The Shulammite woman concludes this section by declaring that love is indestructible. It is true; it is real. Love must be nurtured and developed between two people. It is not easy and it cannot be bought for any price. Unfortunately, there are many husbands and wives out there who try to do exactly this: purchase their spouse's love. There is no gift, no material possession, that can compensate for emotional intimacy in a marriage. In truth, out of everything we have discussed, in many ways true emotional intimacy is the scariest type of intimacy there is, which also makes it the most powerful.

> **Take Action:**
> Do you and your husband share true emotional intimacy? Is your relationship one in which you can both feel safe being completely emotionally raw with one another? Can you trust each other explicitly without fear of being shamed or hurt later? If not, I encourage you to sit down this week and talk about ways to increase your emotional intimacy. If it would be beneficial, there is no shame at all in seeking out a Christian counselor to help you get back on track. Your marriage is worth it.

Chapter 12
Happily Ever After

Before You Begin:
Think back over the text and consider how active the Shulammite woman has been regarding their sexual relationship. While Solomon has been very attentive and romantic, the majority of blatant requests to make love have come from the Shulammite. In fact, as we will soon see, the entire book ends with the Shulammite asking Solomon to make love to her. Does this surprise you? What can you learn from the Shulammite woman regarding sexual intimacy in your own marriage?

Throughout the Song of Songs, we have seen Solomon and the Shulammite's courtship, wedding, and the early years of their marriage. We have seen them rejoice in each other and their love and make careless mistakes that pushed each other away. We have seen them reconcile and make time for each other and return all the stronger for their struggles. At this point, the Shulammite woman's brothers are taking us back to the very beginning. By doing so they lay the foundation of the entire relationship. What made their marriage so successful? How were they able to work through their problems? In His wisdom, God has provided these answers for us!

> **Read Chapter 8:8-9**

Many translations attribute this section to "others;" however, the context makes it clear that the speakers are actually the Shulammite's brothers (see 1:6). Her brothers are remembering back to a time when they were watching their sister grow and mature. They felt a great sense of responsibility for her and a strong desire to protect her and her purity. Even before she began to develop as a woman, her brothers were considering how to help her remain pure. They are saying that if she is a wall––meaning if she is guarding her purity and not easily seduced by men––they will praise her for her strength and purity on the day of her wedding. However, if she is a door (meaning one inclined to chasing after the fellas), they will build a wall around her themselves and lock her away.

Think About It:

- Do we see the purity of our children as a family affair today, or do we largely leave them to their own devices, assured that we have encouraged them to remain sexually pure? How can we better "build a wall" around our children to guide them in remaining pure? What are your thoughts on things such as: teaching them to maintain a pure heart from an early age, chaperoning rather than allowing alone time with the opposite sex, filters on devices, etc.?

- In this text, it is clear that a woman who was easily seduced, or distracted by men, was frowned upon at this time. Yet we seem to praise our young people when they are "popular" with the opposite sex. Do you believe this has attributed to the large number of children reared in the church who are becoming sexually active? How can we, as congregations, better address this?

Read Chapter 8:10-12

Here the Shulammite responds to her brothers' words. Throughout this entire section, she is thanking them and acknowledging the care they took of her. She's reminding them that their concerns were unfounded, because, even as she developed a womanly figure, she remained a wall, closed until her love was awakened by her husband. It has appeared throughout the entire text that the Shulammite woman's family was working one of Solomon's vineyards, which is how they met. Here the Shulammite is drawing a comparison with the actual vineyard that they worked and herself. She is saying that both were cultivated and protected for Solomon. That she is fully his now, yet her brothers still deserve praise and appreciation for all they have done for them both in helping her to remain pure.

Read Chapter 8:13-14

The Shulammite has been contemplating all of this while out in the peace of a garden. She clearly loves her family and leaving them behind has been a struggle for her throughout the entire text. She's remembering all that her brothers did for her and imagining that they miss her and would love to see her (hear her voice) again. Solomon understands what is on her heart and mind and reminds her that, even after everything, he still longs for the simple pleasure of hearing her voice. This beautiful book ends in perfect fashion, as the Shulammite woman responds to her love by asking him to make haste, to come to the mountain of spices, and make love to her.

We have now had an up-close and personal look into the intimate details of Solomon and the Shulammite woman's marriage. It is not a perfect Disney fairy tale, but rather a true and honest glimpse into what it takes to make life work with another imperfect human being. So how were they able to find their happily ever after? I believe that there are a few basic principles that this couple held to, which allowed them to have a fairy-tale marriage in even when faced with the difficulties of life.

#1 – While God is not specifically mentioned anywhere in the text, I believe that Solomon and the Shulammite based their marriage on godly principles. This is evidenced by the emphasis given to sexual purity and the sacrificial, selfless love demonstrated by both throughout their marriage. They embodied Philippians 2:3, "Do nothing from selfish ambition or conceit, but in humility count others more significant than yourself." They did not seek their own in their relationship, but rather they were each focused on meeting the needs of the other. If you'll remember, the one time they failed to do this (when Solomon came to her late at night and she ignored him), it did not bode well for their relationship. Yet in focusing on each other, they were able to quickly rectify the rift between them and emerge with their relationship stronger than before.

#2 – They had a deep awareness of their own needs and struggles, and how they interwove with the needs/struggles of their spouse. From the very beginning both acknowledged that leaving her country home and entering court life would be difficult for the Shulammite woman. Throughout the book we see the Shulammite remaining aware of this and refocusing on Solomon when that inner conflict would arise; however, we also see Solomon being consistently considerate of the Shulammite's struggle by trying to make her as comfortable as possible at the palace and frequently taking her home to visit. Oftentimes in marriage, without realizing it we "kick" each other. What I mean is this: My husband does not meet an expectation I have of him (even if I've never *verbalized* this expectation to him) so I feel unloved. I say, "*If* you loved me..." which triggers his fear of being a bad husband, causing him to be upset and withdraw from me emotionally. This once again triggers my fear of being unloved, and so on. Before we know it, we have entered a destructive cycle of triggering each other's deepest fears and insecurities. Solomon and his bride were able to avoid this by being open and honest about how they felt and why, and then putting out intentional effort to avoid hurtful words/actions and by intentionally building up/encouraging each other in the areas in which they struggled the most.

#3 – They had active communication. While this is primarily a book about sexual love, pause and consider how much verbal communication took place throughout the book. Solomon and the Shulammite woman are both constantly talking about their feelings, their love for each other, their concerns and their struggles. Oftentimes in marriage, we bottle things or shove them down rather than talking and working through them when they first arise. Through open communication Solomon and the Shulammite were able to get straight to the heart of their issues rather than spinning their wheels endlessly trying to figure out what the problem was. Unfortunately, we have several generations of men who were reared that "real men don't talk about their feelings." At the same time, we have generations of passive-aggressive women who nag, belittle, and insult their husbands to the extent that it is no longer emotionally safe to speak openly about their emotions even if they wanted to. Open and sincere communication is a must for a marriage to make it happily ever after. (More on this in the next lesson.)

#4 – They regularly enjoyed true sexual intimacy. When they made love, it was much more than a physical interaction. They regularly included eye contact, romance, and verbal praise in their lovemaking. With this level of mental and emotional intimacy, their sexual intimacy was able to reach a level that we often neglect in our hustle-and-bustle lives. It is easy for sex to become a habitual act to "get through" rather than the true sexual intimacy God intended. We, as both husbands and wives, need to slow down and truly enjoy and appreciate the beautiful gift God has given us in the sexual relationship.

#5 – They both made their marriage a priority. Throughout the entire book, Solomon and the Shulammite woman pursued each other emotionally, romantically, and sexually. They longed to converse with each other. They were attuned to and focused on each other's needs. Solomon was attentive to romancing his wife, creating romantic environments and showering her with praise and admiration, while she was active and creative in pursuing him sexually. They also regularly made time to go away together, to escape from the demands and chaos of everyday life and spend time focusing on each other and their relationship. In today's society, it is not uncommon for couples to divorce after 30+ years of marriage. Why is this? They are so distracted with their children and careers that, by the time the kids leave home, they don't know each other anymore. Our children will be in our homes for 18 years (give or take), but our husbands will be with us until death parts us. We must put out the effort to make our marriages a priority and to make sure those around us know that our marriages are a priority. (Along these lines, actions do speak louder than words! It does us no good to say that our marriage is a priority if our time and effort are consistently focused on other areas!)

The question then becomes, what about us? Are we actively incorporating these five areas into our marriages? What areas are our marriages strong in? What areas do we need to work on? As individuals in the marriage, where are our strengths and weaknesses? Through His infinite wisdom, God has provided us this detailed look into what He desires for our marriages. It is our job to actively conform our marriages to this example, so that we might glorify God through the most important relationship we have on this earth.

Take Action:
Take time this week to sit down and honestly discuss your marriage with your husband. How do you each feel you are doing in these five areas? Do you both believe that you are truly glorifying God in your marriage, or are there improvements that need to be made? Pray together for your marriage, that God will guide and strengthen you as individuals, and as a couple, as you strive to make your marriage all that He would have it be.

Chapter 13
After "I Do:" Barriers to Intimacy

Over the past 12 lessons we have engaged in an in-depth and detailed look at the marriage of Solomon and the Shulammite woman. Through this study we have learned a great deal regarding God's plan for marriage and His intent for us to actively pursue our spouses. While this has been enlightening and beneficial, there are some specific struggles that have not been directly addressed by the text. In our final lesson, we will take a Biblical approach to common struggles experienced after "I do." I have also included a list of recommended reading at the end of the lesson. I pray that this information will be beneficial; however, if you are really struggling in your marriage, I highly recommend that you and your husband invest in time with a Christian counselor.

Question #1 – *My husband and I have different sex drives; what do we do?*

First of all, understand that this is a very common problem in marriages. It is also important to understand that this is a problem that frequently changes throughout a marriage. As we and our husbands age, as we experience pregnancy, etc., our hormone levels change. At one point in your marriage your husband's sex drive may be a lot stronger than yours, only to find that years down the road it switches, and your drive is a lot stronger than his. In this situation we really need to remember 1 Corinthians 7:1-5. As husbands and wives, we are not to withhold sexual intimacy from each other. Regardless of which side of this issue we are on, we need to make sure we are respecting the sexual needs of our spouses as God would have us to. With that being said, here are some practical tips to help with this issue.

For the spouse with the less active sex drive:

- If you have trouble being "in the mood" or making time for sexual intimacy with your spouse, schedule at least one night a week where you both know you will be intimate. If you know it's coming, you have time to prepare emotionally and physically for your spouse. Make it a night where it's fairly easy to get to bed at a decent time so that you really have time to focus on each other.

- Be proactive with your thoughts! Our brains are our largest sex organ. Think about your spouse and how much pleasure he brings you, see what creative ideas you can think of to add variety to your love making. Focus your thoughts on his physical attributes that you find most appealing and thank God for blessing you with your spouse.

- Whether it's your "scheduled" night or hubby surprises you with wanting sexual intimacy, take the time to physically prepare yourself. I promise, he won't mind waiting an extra 30 minutes to an hour! Do whatever makes you feel attractive and relaxed: Take a bubble bath and focus your thoughts on being intimate with your husband, put on makeup and/or lingerie--you'll find that even if sex wasn't on your radar before, you can't wait to be with your man!

- Be very careful with your "No's." Being married does not change the fact that it makes us very vulnerable to express sexual desire. The truth is, if we continually tell our husbands "no" rather than putting forth the physical/emotional effort to meet their needs, they will eventually quit asking. This likely means that either they have completely shut down that aspect of themselves (how horrible!), or they have found a way to get that need met through pornography or a relationship outside of the marriage. Sisters, please do not crush this beautiful aspect of how God made your husbands and what He intended for marriage to be!

- If a "No" is necessary, make sure to set a time when the answer will be "Yes." At this point, it is vital to honor this commitment, otherwise your spouse will have been rejected not once, but twice.

- Initiate! When you are in the mood, let your spouse know! Nothing will build your husband's confidence like knowing that you desire him!

For the spouse with the more active sex drive:

- As difficult as this might be, don't be demanding with your desires. If you continually pressure your spouse to have sex with you, it can easily lead to resentment. Talk openly with your spouse about your needs and find a compromise that will work for both of you. Within that agreement, feel free to show your spouse that you desire them, but be willing to accept it and not take it personally if your spouse does not want to be sexually active every time that you do.

- Focus on meeting your spouse's emotional needs and embrace non-sexual intimacy. It's very difficult to engage in sexual intimacy if you don't feel that your spouse is concerned with meeting your needs. Talk with your spouse and make sure you understand what makes he or she feel the most special and loved, and then do it!

- Set the mood! Plan date nights for you and your spouse. If you have small children find someone to keep them or put them to bed early. Play some romantic music, make the bed, light some candles. It can be difficult to feel sexy in a messy bedroom that smells like dirty laundry with kids constantly knocking at the door, so take care of as many of those obstacles as you can.

- Give your spouse time to prepare physically and emotionally. If you are "in the mood" and he or she isn't, agree to wait 30 minutes to an hour, giving him or her time to prepare so that you can both fully enjoy each other.

For both:

- Keep the romance in your relationship! Make sure that time alone together, even if it's just 1-2 hours after the kids go to bed, is a priority.

- Flirt with each other! Send each other flirty text messages throughout the day, call each other when you can, or put little notes around for them to find.

- Initiate! A healthy sexual relationship in marriage will never be one-sided. Be creative in your sexuality, but make sure to never do anything that violates the other's conscience or makes either one feel unsafe physically or emotionally.

- Talk openly about each other's sexual needs and do your best to make sure you are each having your needs met.

Question #2 – *Help! One of us is addicted to pornography!*

Matthew 7:27-28 makes it clear that lust is unacceptable in God's eyes. Pornography is nothing more than lusting over complete strangers through images. (As a side note, trashy romance novels are female porn and just as damaging to relationships!) While it is not the same as an affair (the word used for "sexual immorality" in Matthew 19:9 carries with it the specific connotation of an actual, physical act with another person), the emotional pain of learning that your spouse is addicted to pornography is earth-shattering. As another side note, this problem is becoming increasingly common among women, not just men. If you are in this situation, here are some practical tips to help you with the healing process.

For the addicted spouse:
- Talk openly and honestly with your spouse about this struggle and how it impacts you and makes you feel.

- Recognize that this is an addiction, and that as an addition you will probably not be able to overcome this on your own. Be humble enough to seek out help.

- It is wise for the addicted spouse to find an accountability partner, preferably a trusted Christian, and then join an accountability group such as Covenant Eyes. This program automatically sends a report of all your online activity to your accountability partner every single week.

For the spouse who is not addicted:
- Talk openly and honestly with your spouse about this struggle and how it impacts you and makes you feel.

- Understand that this is an addiction that changes the chemical functions in the brain. In many ways its effect on chemicals/hormones is similar to that of heroin. It is realistic to expect the addicted partner to struggle with letting go and they may engage in this behavior again as they strive to overcome its addictive nature. It will take some major changes for this to be prevented, a relapse does not necessarily mean that your spouse does not care or is not trying.

- Read *Shattered Vows: Hope and Healing for Women Who Have Been Sexually Betrayed* by Debra Laaser.

For both:

- Both spouses should read: *God, Men and Sex* and *Every Man's Battle*. This helps not only the addicted spouse understand their behavior, but these books provide great insight for both spouses on the impact that pornography has on our brains, as well as practical tips for overcoming this addiction.

- Share electronic accounts such as Facebook and e-mail. If you don't want to go so far as sharing accounts, both spouses should have complete access to every single electronic account, unless this is prohibited by confidentiality with employment.

- The addicted spouse needs to become an open book. An addiction to pornography can shatter trust in the marriage relationship. The best way to rebuild it is to bring everything into the light of day. The addicted spouse needs to allow the other spouse to go through devices, wallets, etc. at any time to prove that he or she has nothing to hide. You cannot rebuild trust in a relationship while hiding things. *A word of caution*-- while this openness can be tremendously beneficial in rebuilding trust in the relationship, it is also vital that the offended party not become his or her spouse's "warden." Checking in on your spouse's activity on occasion to gain peace of mind is one thing; however, it is important to guard against obsessively checking everything your spouse does. The goal is to rebuild trust and gain peace of mind, not search endlessly for more "evidence" to use against your spouse. If your focus and intent is to "catch" him or her, you cannot be focused on rebuilding the relationship.

Question #3 – *Is sex really emotional for my husband, because sometimes it seems like it's just physical?*

Dr. Willard F. Harley's book *His Needs, Her Needs* provides tremendous insight in this area (49-65). If we aren't careful, it is easy for us begin feeling that our husbands are "pawing" at us or that they "only have one thing on their mind." The truth is that, in many ways, sex really does mean "I love you" to many men. Throughout Scripture we see many men doing really dumb things due to their desire for a woman (think Sampson and David). This happens because their emotions are so tied to their sexuality, so as wives we need to be sure we are meeting that desire in our husbands. In fact, the Song of Songs is an excellent example of the emotional meaning that a healthy sexual relationship carries for men. Each man will be different so have open, honest conversations with your husband about what sex means to him and what he really needs from you. For most men, they have a tremendous need to be needed/wanted by their wives, not only sexually but in all areas of life.

Several years ago, my husband and I went through a tremendous time of conflict. He was very busy and under a great deal of stress, so I decided to "help" him. I quit asking him to get high things or open jars, I started taking out the trash and mowing the lawn, everything I could think of to make his life "easier." Unfortunately for him, what I meant to be "easier" really made him feel unneeded. Allow your husband the blessing of helping you and serving you in ways that are valuable to him. At the same time, find out what your husband's love language is, and then speak it! In just a few minutes online, you and your spouse can learn what really "speaks" love to each other. Go to www.5lovelanguages.com and find out.

Most men also need to know that their wives desire them sexually. Show your desire by initiating lovemaking and tell him that you desire him and he brings you pleasure during intimacy and at other times as well! For most men, they can never hear that enough! Communicate with him about what you enjoy most and what brings you the most pleasure, so that he can know he is pleasing to you. And remember, your brain is your largest sex organ! Most wives that I know have something they don't like about their physical appearance: too much weight, wrinkles, too much gray, etc. He loves *you*––he isn't focused on that! For your husband, "sexy" is more about our attitude toward him and lovemaking than it is about your physical appearance. Your husband loves you––he chose you––let him enjoy you!

Question #4 – *My husband has poor hygiene and it makes it difficult to be intimate. What do I do?*

For most people, smell is a tremendous turn-on (or off!) Just consider how often we have seen Solomon and the Shulammite incorporate the sense of smell into their lovemaking! In his book *His Needs, Her Needs*, Dr. Willard F. Harley identifies an attractive spouse as one of the top 10 emotional needs of most individuals (118). Without a doubt, personal hygiene makes a tremendous impact on an individual's attractiveness. First of all, it is human nature to withdraw from things that smell unpleasant. This is the case even when we dearly love the source of that smell.

At the same time, it's human nature to respond when people put out effort for us. My husband loves facial hair, and I hate it. It makes my heart go pitter-patter every time he shaves, because I know that's something that is against his preference, but he does it just to be appealing to me. When we are going to have a date night and we each put out extra effort to look (and smell!) nice, it starts our evening off on a wonderful note. We both automatically feel loved and special because of the effort that has been put out for us. So, if you are in a situation where personal hygiene seems to be more important to you than to your spouse, what do you do? Here are some practical tips.

- First of all, when things are calm and there has not been recent conflict, have an open and honest conversation about this with your husband. Do *not* say, "Honey you stink. Go take a shower!" Do share with your husband how special it makes you feel when he puts out extra effort for you. Tell him that little things, like showering, cologne, brushing his teeth, mouthwash, etc. can truly make you feel like queen of the world because of the special effort he is putting forth just for you.

- Second, our memories are significantly tied to our sense of smell. Make it a fun adventure with your spouse to have special "smells" for your time together. You can go as simple or as far with this as you would like! Have special cologne and perfume, maybe even toothpaste and mouthwash, body wash etc. that are specifically for special times between you and your spouse. These are the special scents you pull out for date night, or when you want to be intimate with each other. You will find that, in time, these scents alone are enough to

Chapter 13 After I Do: Barriers to Intimacy

get you in the mood! You can "plan" your time together and be more spontaneous both! That special cologne or perfume sitting on the bathroom counter can be a sign for you each of what you have to look forward to later that night!

- Third, another little trick is to keep breath mints and candles in your nightstand. Regardless of hygiene practices, no one has good-smelling morning breath! Especially if you are in a time crunch but want to start your day on a high note with your spouse, bedside mints, candles, and body spray can be a lifesaver!

- Finally, do all you can to create a clean, peaceful environment. Make sure you and the kids are showering and brushing your teeth every day, keep the laundry done and smelling as fresh as possible, try not to let dishes pile up in the sink, etc. If the overall tone of the home is clean and peaceful, anyone not engaging in good hygiene will likely feel a little out of place in time.

Question #5 – *How do we overcome struggles from one of us being sexually active before marriage?*

This is a difficult, personal, and utterly common issue among Christian couples today, both in those who were and were not raised in the Lord's church. Here are some practical tips for overcoming this struggle: (as a side-note, this painful situation is powerful information to share with our children when talking to them about remaining pure!)

If you are the one who was sexually active:

- Be honest with your spouse. If this is not something your spouse is aware of, it is a secret that can drive a wedge between you. Talk openly with your spouse but be willing to give him or her time to grieve. This will be an emotional trauma for him or her. Along these lines, while this is something that happened in the past, be prepared for this to damage the trust in the relationship and be patient with your spouse while he or she works towards rebuilding his or her trust in you. For you, this happened long ago, but remember that your spouse will be experiencing it in the here and now. Also, be cautious with how you disclose this information. It would be wise to consider seeing a counselor to help you share this with your spouse in a way that is as least traumatic for him or her as possible. A professional counselor will also be able to help you both communicate openly and honestly as you each work through the emotional impact of this news.

- Make sure you have cut off those old relationships. Learning that your spouse was sexually active with someone in college that they have not spoken to or thought of in years is one thing. Learning that your spouse was sexually active with an individual you play cards with on the weekend is something entirely different! Particularly in regard to social media, let those people go so you can focus on your spouse.

- Focus on your spouse! If we do not guard ourselves, it's human nature to bring back memories of past experiences and even compare. Be totally devoted to your spouse in your heart, mind, and body. Don't let memories of past experiences creep in on you! When you are being intimate with your spouse, focus on your spouse! Look in his or her eyes and fill your mind with all the love and pleasure he or she gives you.

- Compliment your spouse. Tell him continually that you love him, that he is wonderful, and that you enjoy your intimate relationship.

- Don't diminish your spouse's feelings of hurt and betrayal. You might feel this is unfair because it was in the past, but he or she is very much experiencing this in the present emotionally. Give him or her the freedom to do so, without making him feel guilty for hurting, and without telling him all the reasons he "shouldn't" feel the way he does.

If your spouse is the one who was sexually active:

- Be open and honest about how this makes you feel. Don't be accusatory; this is something that happened in the past. But at the same time help him understand that you are hurting and why and guide him through how he can help you overcome this. Be honest about any insecurities this brings up in you, and how he can help assuage those insecurities.

- If he or she has never given you any reason to question his or her dedication to you, don't assume that this new information changes that. Questions of, "Are you thinking of *them*?!" in the middle of lovemaking can destroy the intimacy in a relationship. He is with you, he chose you, he is focused on you, so let him.

- Believe them when they compliment you. Don't create a competition that most likely doesn't exist between you and someone else in your mind.

- Let it stay in the past; bringing it up will only serve to take your spouse's attention off of you and direct it to someone else.

Question #6 – *My husband and I just can't get on the same page. What's going on?*

While not always the case, frequently when we are struggling to be on the same page as our spouses, at the root of our problems are our expectations. For example, early on in our marriage I was very hurt that the grass kept getting taller and taller, and my husband wasn't doing anything about it! He was going to school full-time and working full-time, and he was hurt and frustrated that I kept complaining about the lawn and I wouldn't do anything about it! After a summer of bickering and resentfulness, we finally realized the problem: I grew up in a home where it was assumed that my dad would take care of the outside, and my mom would take care of the inside. He grew up in a single-parent home where any and all chores were done by whoever had the time whenever they had the time. It was a classic case of predetermined expectations. Once we realized the problem, we were able to have an excellent conversation and work out a compromise regarding who would mow the lawn.

In our pre-marital counseling, my husband and I have a list of

Chapter 13 After 'I Do': Barriers to Intimacy   121

114 questions we received from the late minister Tony Hall, and we have the couple fill it out separately. These questions range from who will take out the trash, who will pay the bills and balance the budget, to how many children they will have and what type of discipline they will use. Unfortunately, couples frequently get married without having even considered many of these situations. What happens then is that when their individual pre-determined expectations go unmet, they are frustrated and unsatisfied in their relationship, and may even feel that their spouses don't love them! Sit down with your spouse and come up with a list of as many things as you can that might be an area of pre-determined expectations for you and your spouse. Once you've made up your list, each of you answer the questions on your own, and then come together and compare your answers. Where do you each have predetermined expectations? Are those expectations fair and realistic? How can you compromise in these areas to help strengthen your relationship?

Question #7 – *We just had a baby; how can we balance being parents and spouses?*

This is a struggle that has grown to epidemic proportions in Christian families in America. At this year's American Association of Christian Counselors conference, in a lecture entitled "Attractions, Affairs and Addictions: Preventing 21st Century Marital Destruction," a therapist named Dave Carder presented decades of research demonstrating that 50% of affairs in the greater Christian community in the United States begin during pregnancy or the months immediately following. Sisters, that is a staggering statistic!

I believe that one reason for this is that, as women, if we are not diligent, we struggle with our priorities while bringing a new life into this world. We are exhausted, we don't feel good, our breasts hurt (and are being used as nourishment for a tiny person much of the time), and what little energy we have is being demanded by the precious cries of our little one. Our husbands are big boys, grown men who certainly don't cry for our attention, who are supportive of the mammoth role this new little person will have in our world from now on, so they sit back, quietly supportive, while we and our new little bundle of joy create a new life together. While a new baby absolutely needs our love and attention, this can be a fatal behavior pattern for a variety of reasons.

First of all, this is setting a horrible precedent for our husbands' role in the life of our children. Most of us subscribe to the Biblical pattern of male leadership in the home (Ephesians 5:22-33). Yet as I have heard many say in recent years: Rules without relationship leads to rebellion. What does that mean? Simply that when all Dad is good for is laying down the law, without having adequate time invested in building a relationship with his children, it will be the natural inclination of the children to resent those rules and rebel later in life. Particularly if we are nursing, we are going to have plenty of time to bond with our precious little ones. We need to make sure that we are helping Dad start off on the right foot with this soul he is accountable for by giving him time to bond with the child as well. Encourage Dad to share in the tasks of changing diapers, rocking to sleep, and feeding the baby when possible. Mom, whether Dad feels included and secure in his place in the family or excluded and resentful of your time largely depends on you and your attitude towards him when you have a new little one in your home. Make sure that you are encouraging a parental partnership from the very beginning, and that Dad feels included and has a chance to bond with his child as much as you do.

Second, if we aren't careful, we set a horrible precedent for the future of our marriage. Dave Carder shared his research that pregnancy/infancy is a volatile time for marriages. It's no secret that another volatile time for marriages is the empty-nest period. Why? Because if we aren't careful, we focus so much on our children that we neglect our marriage relationship and the needs of our spouses. Our husbands want to be good husbands, they want us to be happy, they want to be good fathers. They often view us as the "expert," so if we (verbally or otherwise) tell them that they aren't needed and aren't important, they are likely going to "stay out of our way." Unfortunately, oftentimes this leads to us focusing so much on the needs of ourselves and our babies that we completely neglect the needs of our husbands.

Sisters, we can *not* quit being a wife, just because we have become a mother! Our husbands won't cry and demand our attention the way a new baby will, but that does not make their needs any less important! We must make time for intimacy a priority during pregnancy and the months after having a baby. There will be times that sexual intimacy will not be possible due to medical limitations, etc.; however, this can be a great time to focus on the emotional intimacy in our marriages. It can also be a great time to unselfishly focus on your husband and his physical needs. There are ways to bring him pleasure and make sure he knows he is your priority without violating doctor's orders––be creative! Another popular saying is that the best thing we can do for our children is to love our spouses. Sisters, let's love our spouses during this phase of life!

So, we see the need, but it's so hard! What are some practical ways we can do this?

- When the exhaustion sets in, encourage your spouse to watch the baby while you take a nap or soak in the tub. This meets your need for rest, gives you energy to help you meet his needs, takes some of the parenting pressure off of you, and gives him a wonderful opportunity to bond with his child.

- Don't be afraid to ask for help! You are *not* a bad mother if you have family or friends watch your little one so that you and your spouse can spend time focusing on each other.

- Particularly if your little one is sharing your room with you for the time being, get creative with where you are intimate! If a sleeping baby beside the bed is an issue, go to the living room for some one-on-one time.

- If you are a nursing mama, try to pump some milk so that Dad can also have the precious bonding experience of feeding his child. This will ensure that Dad can meet all of baby's needs while you can relax and rest physically, mentally, and emotionally.

- Talk, talk, talk! During this transitional time, it is *so* important to have open, honest communication with your spouse! Talk openly about how you are both adjusting to this change, and what you need from each other. Be open about how you are both feeling as a spouse and as a parent.

In Conclusion:

Throughout the past 13 lessons, we have engaged in an in-depth look at the relationship between Solomon and his Shulammite bride as recorded for us in the Song of Songs. We have seen how they kept their marriage strong and intimate, as well as careless mistakes that they each made and how they were able to restore the intimacy to their relationship afterward. We have seen that God in His infinite wisdom designed the marriage relationship to be full of pleasure and passion and a true bonding of two people, two lives, together. We have seen that, in order for a marriage to be all that God designed it to be, we must be intentional in the pursuit of our spouses. So now, sister, the challenge comes to you! Pursue! May God bless you as you strive to be the wife and mother that He would have you to be.

Recommended Reading

Here is a list of resources that I have found to be helpful, both in my own marriage and in the marriages with whom I have counseled. Keep in mind that while most of these are written by individuals who profess a faith in Christ, they are written by men. These books contain very practical tips that can be incredibly beneficial to your marriage; however, *always* check what you read in light of God's Word.

His Needs, Her Needs: Building An Affair-Proof Marriage by Dr. Willard F. Harley. This book is a fantastic overall guide for marriages. Dr. Harley bases his book on the premise that all people have 10 foundational emotional needs, and when we don't meet those needs for our spouses, we leave them vulnerable to having an affair. He describes and helps the reader identify their needs, as well as explaining the important concept of the "Love Bank."

Fighting for Your Marriage by Drs. Howard Markman, Scott Stanley, and Susan Blumberg. This is the book version of PREP (Prevention and Relationship Enhancement Program.) It is a fantastic program that provides step-by-step ways to improve communication (not only in marriage, but in all relationships), helps couples identify the hidden issues that are feeding their struggles, and improve their problem-solving skills. This book also comes with an educational DVD of therapists working with couples on the skills taught in the book.

Intended for Pleasure by Ed Wheat, M.D. and Gaye Wheat. This book is an excellent resource for Christian couples who are struggling to make the transition to being sexually active after marriage. It provides detailed, practical explanations on a variety of sexual issues. It also provides practical tips on how to remain sexually active during and after pregnancy.

Every Man's Battle: Winning the War on Sexual Temptation One Victory at a Time by Stephen Arterburn and Fred Stoeker with Mike Yorkey. This book specifically focuses on helping men overcome their struggles with pornography. However, I highly recommend all couples read it even if pornography is not a specific struggle for them. It provides great insight on how men's brains process sexual information, and ways we can help protect our husbands and our sons from sexual temptation.

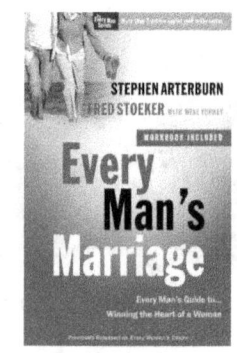

Recommended Reading

Sex, Men and God: A Godly Man's Road Map to Sexual Success by Douglas Weiss. A book to help men develop a three-dimensional (body, mind, and spirit) relationship with their wives. Once again, I also recommend that wives read this book as it provides great insight on how our husbands process sexuality.

Shattered Vows: Hope and Healing for Women Who Have Been Sexually Betrayed by Debra Laaser. Through her own personal experience, Debra shares how women who have experienced sexual betrayal, whether through a one-time incident or an addiction, can heal and emerge stronger than ever before. Debra shares hope and healing for marriages who are hurting due to sexual sin.

The Act of Marriage: The Beauty of Sexual Love by Tim and Beverly LaHaye. Another book that provides practical, descriptive information on how to achieve the beautiful, sexual relationship God intended for us to have in marriage.

Websites:

- http://davecarder.com/. This website has many resources regarding building intimacy in marriage, surviving infidelity,

etc.
- www.5lovelanguages.com. This website is based on the book *The 5 Love Languages* by Gary Chapman.

Bibliography

Arterburn, Stephen, et al. *Every Man's Battle: Winning the War on Sexual Temptation One Victory at a Time.* WaterBrook, 2020.

Chapman, Gary D. *The 5 Love Languages: The Secret to Love That Lasts.* Northfield Pub., 2015.

Dillow, Joseph C. *Solomon on Sex.* T. Nelson, 1979.

Elwell, Walter A., and Barry J. Beitzel. *Baker Encyclopedia of the Bible.* Baker Book House, 1988.

Garrett, Duane A., and E. Ray Clendenen. *Proverbs, Ecclesiastes, Song of Songs* Vol. 14. The New American Commentary: An Exegetical and Theological Exposition of Holy Scripture. Broadman Press, 1993.

Harley, Willard F. Jr. *His Needs, Her Needs: Building an Affair-Proof Marriage.* Flemming H Revell, 2020.

Petrillo, Denny. *Ecclesiastes and Song of Solomon.* Resource Publications, 2016.

www.ingramcontent.com/pod-product-compliance
Lightning Source LLC
Chambersburg PA
CBHW050326120526
44592CB00014B/2065